God's Light: How To Respond

Christian Growth Series

Robert Lloyd Russell

Published by LCL Company NW, 2020.

Also by Robert Lloyd Russell

Bible Character Series
Samson: Spirit-Controlled to Self-Centered
Peter: Failure to Faith

Christian Concepts Series
God's Church: Christ's Pearl
God's Nature: Sonlight Sunlight
God's Child: Like a Tree

Christian Growth Series
God's Desire: How To Please God
God's Light: How To Respond
Christ's Disciple: How To Finish Strong

Christian Theology Series
Christ's Blood: 7+ Amazing Benefits
Pride: Good and Bad
Temptation: 50+ Tips

Table of Contents

God's Light: How To Respond (Christian Growth Series) 1

Reader Responses | & Literary Awards 5

Dedication 9

Preface 11

Dedication 13

Acknowledgements 15

Introduction 17

Prolog: | Heaven Light 21

RESPONSE TO LIGHT: | Application 23

1 | Basic Reactions to Light 25

2 | Absorption: Light Soaked Up 29

3 | Refraction: Light Passed Through 35

4 | Reflection: | Light Bounced Back 43

5 | Opaque: | Provides No Image 51

6 | Translucent: | Provides a Fuzzy Image 57

7 | Transparent: | Provides a Clear Image 65

8 | Summary: | Opaque, Translucent & Transparent 73

9 | Reproduction: | Provides an Accurate Image 77

10 | Substitutes: | Distorted Color 85

11 | Mirages: | Distorted Image 93

12 | Shadows: | Distorted Intensity..99

13 | Luminescence: | Living Light 107

14 | Binary: | One or the Other 115

15 | Result: | Partakers of Light 125

16 | The Bottom Line: | Light Heals! 133

Epilog | The Majesty of Light: | Upward in a Flash 139

About the Author 143

Want Free Books? 145

What To Read Next 147

Bibliography.. 163

While every precaution has been taken in the preparation of this book, the publisher assumes no responsibility for errors or omissions, or for damages resulting from the use of the information contained herein.

SONLIGHT—SUNLIGHT: How To Respond

2021-January-6, 2023-05-08. 23-08-17

Note: This book is an update of the second half of the printed book *GOD LIGHT: Sunlight Sonlight*. The first half was previously released as the eBook *GOD'S NATURE: Sonlight—Sunlight*.

Copyright © 2021 Robert Lloyd Russell

Written by Robert Lloyd Russell

Cover Photo: Public Domain

All Rights Reserved Worldwide ~ Permission granted to quote small portions in any Christian assembly such as for use in preaching, small groups, bulletins, newsletters, and teaching materials when attribution included.

Unless otherwise noted Scripture quotations are from:

NKJV ~ *All Scripture quotations, unless otherwise indicated are taken from the New King James Version®. Copyright © 1982 by Thomas Nelson, Inc. Used by permission. All rights reserved.*

Other Scripture portions as noted are from:

DRB ~ Douay-Rheims Bible, 1899, public domain.

KJV ~ King James Version,1909, public domain

AMP ~ Scripture quotations taken from the Amplified® Bible (AMP), Copyright © 1954, 1958, 1962, 1964, 1965, 1987, 2015 by The Lockman Foundation Used by permission.

NASB ~ Scripture quotations taken from the (NASB®) New American Standard Bible®, Copyright © 1960, 1971, 1977, 1995, 2020 by The Lockman Foundation. Used by permission. All rights reserved.

NIV ~ The Holy Bible, New International Version®, NIV® Copyright © 1973, 1978, 1984, 2011 by Biblica, Inc.™ Used by permission.

GNT ~ Good News Translation® (Today's English Version, Second Edition) Copyright © 1992 American Bible Society. All rights reserved.

TLB ~ The Living Bible copyright © 1971 by Tyndale House Foundation. Used by permission of Tyndale House Publishers Inc., Carol Stream, Illinois 60188. All rights reserved. The Living

NOTES: [1] For consistency and clarity, names and pronouns of God have been capitalized throughout including in Bible versions which do not follow that practice. [2] The author capitalizes three other words: "Word" when speaking of God's Word; "Church" when speaking of the Church universal; and "Cross" when referring to the Cross of Calvary. [3] *Italicized* words and [bracketed words] in Scripture have been added by the author. [4] The author does not abbreviate the names of Bible books since abbreviations can be unknown to some readers. [5] The author chooses to use a lot of Scripture quotations based on his belief that the Word of God and the Spirit of God are the two dominant factors in changing lives and growing the lives of Christians.

We hope you enjoy this book. Robert Lloyd Russell's goal is to provide high-quality, thought-provoking books that connect truth to real life needs and challenges. For more information on his other books based on Biblical interpretation and application, please visit his author's website booksrlr.

If you find value in this book, please consider writing an online review. The author would be grateful.

But if we are living in the light, as God is in the light, then we have fellowship with each other, and the blood of Jesus, His Son, cleanses us from all sin.

1 John 1:7

Reader Responses
& Literary Awards

To the earlier printed version *God Light*

First there was Tozer with *The Knowledge of the Holy,* and then Packer gave us *Knowing God,* and now Russell has taken us further with *God Light*.

There is a tremendous need for a book on this subject. We have witnessed the publication of many books around the statement "God is Love," but I cannot recall ever seeing one around the statement "God is Light." It is important that these two attributes of God be brought into conjunction with each other because it is really impossible to discuss love intelligently without understanding light.

~ Dr. Earl D. Radmacher, General Editor, Nelson Study Bible/New King James Study Bible

This is truly amazing. I marvel at the wisdom God has given you and the talent to put it on paper in a meaningful/fascinating way. I have anything but a scientific mind! I found myself saying out loud, "Wow, that's amazing," many times. I worked through the technical only to be thrilled by the application at the end of each chapter. The parallel of God and His Son to the sun is brilliant! I know it's in God's Word but you have brilliantly explored His message and made it meaningful to an "un-brilliant" person such as myself!

You have opened my eyes to the light around me. Yesterday, as I looked at the clouds casting shadows on the earth, I thought of the truths you have taught me. I look at ordinary things differently. I have already used many of the truths in my mentoring and find myself sharing your thoughts in everyday conversation.

This is so rich! ... This is great! ... Wonderful! ... Mind boggling to say the least! ... Great material for discussion! ... Application pieces are truly inspired!

~ Elizabeth Hightower, Women's Ministries Leader, Laurelwood Baptist Church

He obviously is hitting on all twelve cylinders! What an exciting insight into Christ as the light of the world. Thank God for people like this who have the background to illuminate some of these Biblical concepts.

~ Dr. Joe Aldrich, President, Multnomah Bible College & Biblical Seminary

I was utterly fascinated... I am impressed with the work that you have done, with the directionality it has... I do believe that you have an important message which could be greatly used of the Spirit of God in the world today both among the Christian community and in pre-evangelism of the world.

~ Dr. Ronald Barclay Allen, Senior Professor of Bible Exposition, Dallas Seminary

It is must reading.

~ Richard C. Halverson, Chaplain, U.S. Senate

The content is terrific... This is a timely book... There is so much content that many other books and articles could be written from small parts of it.

~ Dr. Freeman L. Schmitt, Senior Pastor

I got so involved in the subject and read with such great interest that I had trouble reading it critically for accuracy.

~ Maury J. Merrick, Optics Professor & Consultant

I find it most inspirational. I can't profess to knowing anything of physics, never having studied the subject: but the explicit way in which you describe it all – I feel I am able to understand... You make the reader think, and that is a great talent.

~ Evelyn Cox, homemaker

I loved the book *God Light*! ... It is very well written and very understandable. Without seeming condescending or talking down to anyone he gets the point across. The Josh McDowell book, *Evidence That Demands a Verdict,* is good too... as soon as I finish it I plan on reading *God Light* again. It is definitely the better of the two.

~ Bobby Glasgow, inmate

AWARDS

Gold Medal Winner, Christian Non-Fiction, *2013 Readers' Favorite* Award.

Winner, Religion—Non-Fiction, *Beverly Hills Book Award.*

Reviewers Choice Award, Religion—Eastern/Western, *2012 Reader Views Award.*

Best Book, Religion—Christianity, *2012 World Book Award.*

Runner-Up, Religion—Christianity, *2012 USA Best Book Awards.*

Finalist, Book—Biblical Studies, *2013 The Word Guild* (Canada).

Dedication

To all God's children

who are striving

for Christian maturity.

Preface

This eBook is an updated version of Part 3 of an earlier print book *"GOD LIGHT: Sunlight Sonlight."* Parts 1 and 2 of that book have been updated and published as an eBook entitled *"GOD'S NATURE: Sonlight Sunlight"* (ISBN: 978-1393359371). It compares aspects of natural physical light with the attributes of the Son of God. While it is not a prerequisite to read that eBook first, it may be helpful to some readers.

|||||| ||||||

Starting a new position is always a challenge—but this time I was in foreign territory. I had been named Camera Engineering Manager of a Fortune 500 firm. Although I possessed engineering management experience and was an avid amateur photographer, I knew virtually nothing about optics and the theories of light. It was a time of intense technical study.

Simultaneously I became intrigued with the Apostle John's statement in 1 John 1:5 that "God is light." What did John mean? Is there something more to this statement than meets the eye? Did the Holy Spirit of God inspire John to write three simple words that were packed with meaning beyond what John could fully understand? As I studied physical light, these questions remained prevalent in my thinking.

Virtually all Christians would agree that God is love, God is light, and God is life (1 John 4:8, 1:5, 5:12). These three concepts have been acknowledged by hymn-writers and poets for centuries. However, I found it curious that when it comes to books, literally thousands have been written on the subject God is love and on the new life that God makes available, but precious little has been penned about God is light.

In my quest I came to understand that some of the characteristics of physical light help us to understand God's nature and give new meaning to John's phrase, "God is light."

It is significant that when the apostle whom Jesus loved wrote "God is light," he gave us his purpose for writing this epistle in the previous verse, "We write this to make our joy complete." It is my desire that contemplating the nature of God as seen in the Apostle John's statement "God is Light" will bring joy to each reader.

This book may be considered a series of short essays about God light, each essay designed to provoke further thinking. The short chapters are relatively broad strokes of a brush; it is left up to you, the reader, to add details, highlights, and clarification through personal study, prayer, meditation, and life experiences. It is my prayer that such a process will allow truth to be revealed in a new and refreshing way, and in the process, "your joy might be complete."

Dedication

To all God's children

who are striving

for Christian maturity.

Acknowledgements

Many individuals have influenced the direction of this book over the more than a quarter century that I have contemplated the parallels between natural light and spiritual light. (The original manuscript was completed in 1980-82.) Space permits listing only those of greatest influence.

Jim Elliot, the martyred missionary to Ecuador—was my Sunday School teacher as a young boy and a life-long example. Specifically, Jim modeled the need to take responsibility for thinking deeply about spiritual things.

Dr. Earl Radmacher has been a supportive friend and a tremendous encourager over the many years the manuscript has been developed.

Reviewers of the manuscript listed alphabetically include, Bob DeViney, Elizabeth Hightower, Warren and Betty Manley, Dr. Maurie M. Merrick, Sue Parry, and Dr. Earl D. Radmacher.

My daughters Linda and Laura have offered support, encouragement, and illustrations. Years later my then five-year-old granddaughter Abigail wrote the following poem which she entitled "God is Light:"

God loves you and me.

God loves everything.

When we stumble in the darkness

We will see that God is light.

When I am afraid

I will trust in God.

Even when we disobey

God still loves us.

I love God.

I have been truly blessed by a family that has supported me and personally sacrificed throughout many years.

Connie, my wife, has been the single most important person of influence. Her great copy-editing skills, patience, and willingness to offer constructive criticism even when it was not readily received were all essential elements. Without Connie the manuscript would never have become a book.

My sincere thanks to the co-laborers mentioned above and to all the others for providing input, encouragement, and prayer.

Introduction

Sunlight reaches earth every day quietly providing vision, warmth, and sustenance for all life. Meanwhile lightning strikes 1,000 people in the United States each year and ignites 10,000 forest fires. Thunderstorms kill more people in the U.S. than any other natural disaster. Sunshine and gentle wind are taken for granted, but in violent forms natural elements are referred to as "acts of God."

As humans we often do not consider God during good times, but the saying from the First World War has a ring of reality, "There are no atheists in fox holes."

It is important to comment briefly regarding the scientific accuracy of this book and the parallels presented between how science currently understands physical light and what the Scriptures reveal about the God who is light. First, this manuscript has been reviewed by light and optical experts. Although concepts have been simplified for easy reading, the content is accurate according to current scientific knowledge.

Second, the author is aware that scientific understanding changes over time. Therefore, it is quite possible that there may come a time when scientists learn that light does not behave exactly as they believe it does today. Should significant changes in man's understanding of light occur, it is quite possible that some of the material in this book will become dated and perhaps some sections may be found to be inaccurate.

Third and most importantly, if such an event should occur, the reader should rest assured that while our scientific understanding of light has changed, the nature of God has not changed.

Finally, it is my prayer that if such events occur, God will at that time raise up new individuals to help readers of that era understand the mysteries surrounding the God who is light.

A key question which arises then: why take the time to understand parallels between the nature of natural light as scientists understand it and the nature of God as revealed in Scripture?

Dr. Robert John Russell (no relation to this author) has written, "As in bridge building, each community, the religious and the scientific, must find bedrock in its own world, yet each must venture out toward the other, hoping that one day the two will meet at the keystone."[1]

As we understand the marvels of physical light, our understanding of the uniqueness of God light will be greatly enhanced. We will see God in a new and intriguing way.

Sunlight / Sonlight

Sunlight is an essential part of our everyday existence.

Sonlight is an essential part of the everyday existence of the followers of the Son of God.

THINK AND GROW

1. Have you ever thought deeply about physical light?

2. Have you ever thought deeply about spiritual light?

3. Have you heard or read much about the parallels between physical and spiritual light?

Prolog:
Heaven Light

Will it be light or dark in Heaven?" asked my then five-year-old daughter Laura. It was evening and I had just tucked her into bed. As I sat on the edge of her bed, she looked up with an inquisitive innocence that communicated to me that it was a serious question.

We had developed a little game at bedtime; I would ask Laura a question regarding the Bible, and she would provide the answer. It was, I thought, a good way to communicate some Christian truths in a natural way. One of the questions that she never missed was, "What three things that characterize God's nature start with L?" Her response was always immediate, sure, and consistent, "God is love, God is light, and God is life." Because I was sure that she knew these concepts well, it bothered me to have her now pose this question, which to me had such an obvious answer.

Calmly and methodically I began to help Laura discover the answer for herself. "Well, Honey," I began, "what three things characterize the nature of God?" "But Dad," she replied, "you know I know that! What I want to know is will it be light or dark in Heaven?" "Well, Laura, what do you think?" "Dad!" her exasperated soft voice replied. As much as I didn't want to give in and spoon-feed her the answer, I replied, "Honey, since God IS light, don't you suppose it will be very, very light in heaven?"

Laura appeared to be deep in thought for a few seconds and then came her reply, "I thought it would be very, very, dark so that we would be able to see Him better!" I must admit I like her concept better than my own, and to this day when reflecting on that moment I feel a lump in my throat.

Throughout the Bible we find man pictured as being in darkness—more literally "as darkness"—or spiritually blind. Those who have discovered and acted upon the truth of Jesus Christ as the Son of God are pictured oppositely as in the light—literally "as light"—with spiritual sight.

As we begin our study of parallels between sunlight and Sonlight, consider the apparent paradox: it is physically harmful to look directly at the sun, but spiritually necessary to look to the Son for direction and salvation (Numbers 21:8, John 3:14).

As a flower moves itself to face the sun, we should keep our focus on the Son. A.W. Tozer put it this way, "God made us to be like planets. Around and around they go, held together by the magnetic attraction of the sun."

May you always keep the Son in your eyes!

Sunlight / Sonlight

Sunlight dispels physical darkness.

Sonlight dispels spiritual darkness.

THINK AND GROW

What do you think? Will it be light or dark in heaven?

RESPONSE TO LIGHT: Application

The man who will not act until he knows all will never act at all.

Jim Elliot

But if we are living in the light, as God is in the light, then we have fellowship with each other, and the blood of Jesus, His Son, cleanses us from all sin.

1 John 1:7

1

Basic Reactions to Light

What are the different reactions to physical light? What types of reactions are there to spiritual light? Are there any parallels? What can you learn about your reactions to the Son of God from the reactions of objects to sunlight?

In the physical world it is uncommon for an object to react to physical light in only one way. Usually we find a number of complex interacting reactions. The same is true regarding reactions to spiritual light. Therefore, as you read the following material, remember that the chapters are interrelated. There is no way to adequately portray these interdependencies in just a few short chapters. Individual reactions are treated as separate entities to stimulate thought about analogies between the effects of physical light and spiritual light.

In the earlier eBook, *God's Nature: Sonlight Sunlight,* I paralleled the nature of light and the nature of God. Those individual chapters are also far from exhaustive and are interrelated, but there is a significant difference. In that eBook we were dealing with absolutes. The speed of light is an absolute and God is absolutely sovereign. In this follow-up eBook there are few absolutes. For example, this page you are reading absorbs some light while it reflects other light. A given quantity of light reaching this page will warm it more than the same quantity of light reaching an object of the same size made of certain other materials, but less than an object of the same size made of other materials.

The various reactions to light are not absolute and do not have intrinsically positive or negative impacts. The relative impact of a particular reaction to light must be viewed regarding an object's total response to the light. This is not unlike spiritual light. Much of our knowledge concerning spiritual things comes to us from the Word of God, the Bible. While the Bible does contain some absolutes, it is also very much a book of interrelated principles. Many people have erred by taking a single concept or two and emphasizing them beyond the intent of Scripture. The Bible is its own best commentary. To understand any specific passage properly, it must be understood in relationship with its immediate context and with the whole of Scripture.

This book examines the various reactions of objects to sunlight striking them. There are analogies between the effects of sunlight striking a physical object and the effects of Sonlight on human beings. Understanding reactions to physical light will help you understand your reactions to Sonlight.

Analogies are always to be used with caution; they are far from perfect. Sometimes analogies are considered suspect because they are not precise or scientific. That concept of analogies is quite appropriate. However, even the most technical research scientists often pursue avenues of experimentation based on an indication that something reacts in an analogous way to something else. Often it is necessary to have a "first approximation" prior to a more detailed understanding. It is my desire that these analogies, while not to be taken too precisely, will help you to understand your own reactions to Sonlight. As that is accomplished, an increased understanding and respect of how others react to spiritual light will naturally occur.

Sunlight / Sonlight

Physical objects react to sunlight in a variety and combination of ways.

Humans react to Sonlight in a variety and a combination of ways.

THINK AND GROW

1. List some examples of where taking a specific passage from the Bible by itself without considering the rest of Scripture could lead to an incorrect solution.

2. List some examples of where taking a specific natural law or principle without considering other laws and principles could lead to a wrong conclusion.

2

Absorption: Light Soaked Up

In this chapter and the next two we will consider three very basic reactions to light: absorption, refraction, and reflection. For purposes of analogy, think of *absorption* as light being *soaked up*. On the other hand, *refraction* occurs when light is transmitted, or *passed through*. Finally, *reflection,* following the same type of analogy, may be thought of as light *bounced back*. Many objects do all three, that is the light striking them is partially absorbed or soaked up, partially refracted or passed through, and partially reflected or bounced back. Not all objects react in all three ways, but it is rare for an object to have only one of these reactions to light.

All three reactions can be beneficial. On the other hand, given the right circumstances any one of the three reactions could be undesirable. This chapter considers the reaction to light called absorption.

Absorption

Imagine for a moment a man standing on a wide-open sandy beach holding a handgun. He points the gun downward and slowly squeezes the trigger. The bullet enters the sand near his feet and is "absorbed" by the sand.

The principle is the same with the absorption of light. First, notice that the bullet has disappeared into the sand. When light is absorbed, it disappears. When scientists discuss the absorption of light, they know there is a loss of intensity of the light. In fact, the term *absorption* may be thought of as a decrease in intensity. The intensity of light is diminished just as the speed of the bullet was diminished by the sand.

Second, if you were to retrieve the imaginary bullet immediately after it entered the sand, you would discover that it was quite hot. A significant portion of this heat would be from the friction that occurred as the bullet made its way through the sand. When light is absorbed, there is physical heat. We know that light is a form of energy. When light is absorbed, it is transformed from one kind of energy to another kind of energy. Light becomes heat. Scientists often look at this process from just the opposite point of view, that is, if any of the initial light is transformed into heat, they know there has been absorption. The heat came from friction between the bullet and the individual grains of sand. Heat from the absorption of light comes about in the same way. The heat is the result of motion among the molecules which make up the absorbing material. Even though energy is changed from one form to another, it is not consumed. Light is changed to heat, but the energy is indestructible.

When light comes in contact with any *transparent* material, we know that some of the light will be absorbed (soaked up), some will be refracted (passed through), and the remainder will be reflected (bounced back). The total energy of the light before striking the transparent material will equal the total energy of the absorbed light plus the refracted light plus the reflected light.

In the earlier volume entitled *"GOD'S NATURE: Sonlight Sunlight"* we saw that light travels for astronomical distances with apparently no loss of energy. In a vacuum essentially no energy in the form of light is lost. We know therefore that no light is absorbed in a vacuum. However, it is not uncommon for relatively thin dark eyeglasses to absorb over half of the light which enters.

Solar energy is an important and growing source of man's energy. What is the principle involved? Solar collectors of many varieties convert the energy we call light into the energy we call heat. Solar collectors work through absorption. In March of 1981 the United States' first commercial solar power plant became operational, in Crosbyton, Texas. In recent years significant gains have been made in the ability to harness solar energy, but even the most liberal estimates say that only a very tiny fraction is being harnessed. For all of man's sophistication, we do not really have a very complete understanding of light, and we have even less knowledge of how to channel the abundant solar energy all around us into practical man-caused benefits (or the potential adverse effects regarding the balance of creation). It has been estimated that "on every sunny acre, 7,000 horsepower of radiant energy from our solar dynamo is going to waste."[1] It is estimated that the sun bathes our planet with about 10,000 times as much energy each day as we consume in fossil fuels.

There is another significant aspect of absorption. Some materials are quite selective in respect to their absorption of light. A material is said to show *general absorption* if it absorbs all wave lengths, that is all colors, of light nearly equivalently. Other materials are said to show *selective absorption* in that their absorption is only of certain colors. This is a most fundamental aspect of the way many materials react to light. Practically all colored substances, including natural objects, owe their color to their selective absorption. A flower is an example; flowers have *body color* (or show pigment). In contrast, some material objects such as polished gold have *surface color,* which is produced almost entirely by reflected light. In leaves, flowers, and other objects with body color, the sensation we call color is produced by light penetrating the surface and entering some depth into the object. The light that has penetrated is then scattered and reflected, escaping from the surface of the object.

Crater Lake in south central Oregon has been described by many as the bluest lake in the world. Its water is a deep, almost iridescent blue. Those hardy individuals who hike the steep trail down the caldera surrounding the lake discover that the water looks just as blue from the water's edge as it does from high on the rim above the lake. Riding in a boat, your craft appears to be floating in an enormous pool of extremely transparent blue ink.

There are many reasons for Crater Lake's blue water. The color is affected by several external factors, including the time of day and the amount of cloud cover. The primary factor in the blueness, however, is the extreme purity of this very deep lake. As light waves enter the water, the longer light waves (reds, yellows, etc.) are all absorbed; the shorter light waves (blues, greens, etc.) penetrate much further into the water. The shortest wavelength light, that is the blue, continue deeper into the water than the others. These blue rays are eventually scattered and reflected to the surface. Only the blue rays are returned to the surface, causing the lake to appear very blue indeed. If a lake were to absorb all the light, it would appear black to observers. Because of Crater Lake's extreme depth and extreme purity, it absorbs all the light except the blue waves, which are scattered and returned to the surface.

Absorption and scattering are related, but they are distinct. Imagine for a moment that you are driving at night down a lonely highway in a very dense fog. Your headlights are working fine, but you cannot see very far in front of your car. You try the high beams only to discover that you can see even less! The fog is scattering the light from your headlights. Increasing the brightness of the lights only provides a greater intensity of light to be scattered. This is quite a different reaction to light than absorption. Absorption represents the transformation of light into heat. Absorption causes the visual disappearance of light. Scattering causes the light to be bounced around in all directions, making it more visible. In the case of this example, the car headlights are no longer focused on the roadway ahead but are now bounced around among the vapor droplets that form the fog, creating a blinding white wall in front of your headlights.

Application

The single most important aspect of the absorption of light is the generation of heat. This has a spiritual analogy. We have said that reactions to light can be both good and bad, and that is true of absorption. The Word of God brings warmth to your heart and cheers your soul as it is absorbed. Physical light also warms when it is absorbed. But notice that heat is generated when light is absorbed, regardless of the material. The Word of God absorbed by one who is not a Christian also generates heat. This can cause a great deal of unrest and even a figurative running from God. In the physical world the darker the material, the greater the amount of light that will be absorbed—eventually such an object can become hardened and brittle to the point of destruction.

The writer of Hebrews, regarding the sin of unbelief, wrote: "But encourage one another daily, as long as it is called Today, so that none of you may be hardened by sin's deceitfulness" (Hebrews 3:13 niv). As surely as the sun softens butter left on a windowsill, it hardens a piece of bread left beside it. The Son of God, Jesus Christ, is shining forth with the true light, and some individuals are being softened while others, refusing to acknowledge Him, are being hardened. Such an individual needs to turn to God for salvation and then bask in the warmth of His love.

Having acknowledged the true light, what we need to do is analogous to what Crater Lake does. We need to absorb the light, but we also need to scatter some light around our deepest parts, examining ourselves for inner purity; and we also need to return some of the light back outside of ourselves so that others may enjoy its beauty. We need to absorb God's grace, mercy, and justice, as well as understand His hatred of sin and His wrath. But we also need to return some light to others around us regarding God's love, His plan of salvation, His sovereignty, and His personal interest in every individual.

We do not have to understand every aspect of God and His nature in order to benefit from His love. It has only been in comparatively recent history, since the development of the quantum theory, that mankind has gained an acceptable level of understanding of the photographic process. Photography is a complicated process in which electrons absorb the energy of light. It is fortunate that we do not have to fully understand a process in order to apply it in a practical and meaningful way. It would be safe to assume that only a very small portion of the world's amateur photographers could give an accurate and detailed technical description of the process that occurs when light strikes film or in digital camera. That does not, however, undermine the reality of the enjoyment that millions of photographers derive from their photography. So too in spiritual matters, you may not understand all the mysteries of our Creator, but that does not negate the value of heeding His Word and His game plan for your daily living.

Light produces warmth when it is absorbed. In fact, light only warms when it is absorbed. The warmth that comes from being at peace with one's Creator only comes by absorbing the reality and truth of God.

Sunlight / Sonlight

The absorption of sunlight generates heat.

The assimilation of Sonlight generates heat.

THINK AND GROW

Have you acted upon the reality of spiritual light?

3

Refraction: Light Passed Through

Have you ever stood beside a swimming pool and looked at someone standing waist-deep in the water? If the top of the water was smooth and you could see into it, you noticed that the person appeared to be substantially shortened below the water surface. Proportionately that person is an odd sight. The upper portion of the individual, which is above the water, appears quite normal; but the remainder of the individual, the part in the water, appears quite short and wide. This appearance is because of *refraction*.

If you look straight down into clear water, the depth appears less than it really is. The water appears to be only about three-quarters of its real depth. If the surface of the water is smooth so that you can look out at the water, that is not straight down, and still see the bottom, the effect is even greater. It may appear only half its actual depth.

Perhaps you've been on a lake in a rowboat and noticed that as you looked at the oars, they appeared to be bent as they entered the water. Furthermore, as you lowered the oar deeper into the water, the bend always appeared to stay at the surface. This is also a result of refraction.

Whenever light travels through the boundary of two transparent mediums, it changes direction slightly, except when it passes the boundary at a right angle. In both the above examples, light is passing through the boundary of two transparent mediums, air and water. Because of refraction, light changes direction when it crosses such a boundary.

Just like absorption in the previous chapter, refraction can be desirable or undesirable. Refraction can cause light to be very pretty and useful

35

in prisms. But refraction can cause a problem known as chromatic aberration. The color fringing of chromatic aberration in camera lenses and other optical systems presents many challenging problems to optical system engineers.

Refraction causes a bending of the direction which light is traveling. A familiar example of a boundary of two transparent mediums is a window. In the case of a single-pane window, there are two boundaries. During the daylight hours the first boundary light reaches is between the outside air and the outside surface of the glass. The second boundary is between the inside surface of the glass and the inside air. During nighttime hours with interior lights on, the first and second boundaries are reversed. If the window is a dual-pane, insulated type of window, there are four boundaries instead of two, but the principle remains the same.

If light is bent at each of these boundaries, why is it that we do not commonly see distortion of the type mentioned in the two previous examples? The answer is very simple. When the transparent medium is approximately uniform in thickness, at both boundaries the light is bent equally but in opposite directions. The net result is that light is moving in exactly the same direction as it exits the glass as it was when it entered the glass. The only difference is that the light has shifted slightly in position. As you look through a window from an angle, the objects you see are not exactly where they appear to be.

A prism on the other hand behaves quite differently. A prism is a piece of transparent material of non-uniform thickness.

Many prisms, instead of showing the effects of refraction, are used to *reflect* light back in approximately the same direction as the light source. A quality diamond of jewelry grade is an excellent prism. The reflectors that are common on automobile taillights are examples of relatively simple and crude prisms.

Most prisms allow light to be passed through. Since they do not have a uniform thickness, we can expect to see some noticeable effects caused by the bending of light, and we will not be disappointed. As light passes through a prism, an interesting and beautiful effect occurs. Light from our sun is called white light and is made up of many different wavelengths of light. These wavelengths when viewed individually are perceived as colors by humans. As light passes through a prism, the different wavelengths are bent different amounts. Therefore, although "white light" enters the prism, a "rainbow of colored light" emerges from it. Although the visible light rays themselves are not colored, we perceive color through a complex set of reactions with our human eyes and brain. David wrote, "I will praise You because I am fearfully *and* wonderfully made" (Psalm 139:14).

Refraction is so predictable that scientists use their ability to measure the amount of bending that occurs to determine the precise wavelengths of the light entering prisms of known dimensions.

A common but not well-known example of refraction involves the light from our sun. As the light coming through the transparent medium we call outer space enters another transparent medium which we call our earth's atmosphere, the light is refracted. In other words, the sunlight is bent. This effect is greatest at sunrise or sunset and least around noon. The interesting result of this is that we perceive the sun as above the horizon *after* it has gone below the horizon. Therefore, when we are observing the sun setting on the ocean, the sun has already passed below the horizon.

Another interesting effect of the refraction of sunlight as it enters the earth's atmosphere occurs during a total lunar eclipse. During these events no sunlight falls directly on the side of the moon that we see because the earth is directly between the sun and the moon. The earth, which is 5,717 miles in diameter, is about two and one-half times the

2,160-mile diameter of the moon. Yet the moon is clearly visible but appears copper in color. The blue light end of the spectrum has been blocked, while some light waves at the red end have been refracted around the earth's atmosphere—only the red light makes it to the moon. This red light is from the sunrise and sunset glow of earth that is refracted around the earth's rim through our atmosphere. If at the time of an eclipse there is a lot of volcanic dust in the atmosphere, the moon appears dimmer and will be a darker shade of red.

There is a related but different term, called *diffraction*. Refraction is the changing of direction by light as it moves obliquely from one transparent medium to another. On the other hand, *diffraction* is the bending of light as it passes an obstruction. For example, when light passes through a hole, light waves near the edge of the hole spread out instead of continuing in their original direction. The smaller the hole, the more significant is the effect of diffraction. In diffraction, there is no change in mediums through which light is traveling. The amount which light is diffracted is dependent upon the wavelength of the light. The longer wavelengths of light are diffracted a greater amount than the shorter wavelengths.

A simple observation of the effects of diffraction can be made on a bright sunny day when the shadows are reasonably long. Have a friend stand still and then carefully examine the edge of the shadow. At your friend's feet the shadow's edge will be very distinct. Further away from your friend's feet the edge of the shadow will be less distinct. The shadow edge that represents your friend's head will be the least sharply defined of all. Diffraction causes a slight bending of light rays as they pass by a material object. The further away from the point of that bending, the greater will be the divergence of the light rays, causing in this case a less distinct shadow.

A rainbow is another related phenomenon. When droplets of water vapor (a transparent medium) are present in air (another transparent medium) with strong sunlight, a complex reaction to the sunlight occurs which involves both refraction and diffraction. However, the rainbow's colors may be thought of as being formed in a similar fashion to the colors that form when sunlight is passed through a prism.

Application

Refraction is the changing of direction of light waves as the light passes through the boundary of two transparent mediums. The amount of refraction is primarily dependent upon the wavelength of the light and the angle at which the light crosses the boundary.

There is also a reaction to light called *diffraction*, which also causes a change in direction of light. Diffraction occurs as light passes next to a material object. The "silver lining" of clouds under certain conditions is perhaps one of the more common examples of diffraction.

Absorption (previous chapter), refraction (this chapter), and reflection (next chapter) are interconnected reactions. Some objects do all three at once. Each of the three reactions can be desirable or undesirable. Parallels between the reaction to sunlight and the reaction to Sonlight are not clear-cut. We can, however, suggest some ways that we can visualize some similarities, ways in which the reaction to physical light is analogous to reaction to spiritual light.

As a child of light in a dark world, you should allow the full light of the pure life of Christ to be displayed in your lives as a beautiful array of Christian virtues. This suggests a similarity to the way physical light diffuses into a rainbow of colors when it shines through a prism.

David Needham in his marvelous book, "Birthright; Christian, Do You Know Who You Are?" wrote: "Who is a Christian? He is God's ultimate spiritual masterpiece. God's purposed new man. Created clean as a flawless prism, progressively being faceted more fully to receive, transform, and display the otherwise invisible glories of the infinite God into limitless, visible colors—the rainbow of His own attributes—so that all creation might see GOD! This is life. The outflow of meaning. The Divine perfecting of your own truest, deepest, eternal identity. 'But you are a chosen people, a royal priesthood, a holy nation, a people belonging to God, that you may declare the praises of Him who called you out of darkness into His wonderful light.' (1 Peter 2:9 niv)"[2]

This beauty which results from being God's prism in a dark needy world is only possible as we stay in the Light. The apostle Paul reminds us, "But now you are light in the Lord. Live as children of light" (Ephesians 5:8 niv). Without light a prism is a useless thing. "Without light it really isn't much at all—just a hunk of glass. But with light, oh! It reflects all the colors of the rainbow. This, to me, is the most expressive illustration of a Christian that I know. In terms of his deep, spiritual personhood, he is a uniquely designed prism. A prism formed by the Creator to receive His very life (invisible to the world) and translate that light into the visible colors of the character of God. To most fully appreciate my prism, I must hold it in direct line with the sun. I must also choose a good surface to display the resulting colors of the spectrum."[3]

You should be a clean transparent prism in order that others might see the beauties of Christ—who is Light—in us. Your life should display the grace, mercy, peace, hope, holiness, and justice of God.

Sunlight / Sonlight

Sunlight changes direction as it passes through boundaries of materials.

Sonlight causes a change of direction as it penetrates human hearts.

THINK AND GROW

1. Have you experienced a change in direction because of the penetration of Sonlight? If so, write a short paragraph of testimony regarding the changes.

2. Is your life a rainbow of spiritual color?

4

Reflection:

Light Bounced Back

Some basketball players become very adept at banking the ball off the backboard and into the net. The ball is deflected off the backboard and into the basket. When light does a similar thing, we say it is reflected.

Light interacts with material objects in three principle ways. In absorption light is soaked up. In refraction light is passed through. And in *reflection* light is "bounced back."

Remember that refraction occurs when light passes through the boundary of two differing transparent mediums. Reflection occurs when light strikes the boundary of two different mediums and is reflected. These mediums do not need to be transparent.

Objects do not usually react to light in only one of these ways but in two or all three.

There are two main kinds of reflection. A very smooth surface, that is a highly polished surface, produces mirror-like reflections. This is called *specular* or *regular* reflection. Any reflection which provides a clear image as light is reflected off a surface is a specular or regular reflection. This type of reflection is discussed in a later chapter. Most reflective surfaces are relatively rough, causing *diffused* or *irregular* reflections. In this case the reflected light is scattered as it is reflected. The result is that an image cannot be seen in diffused or irregular reflections.

Think about light reflecting off water. Perhaps everyone has at one time or another observed a lake or other body of water that appeared to be "as smooth as glass." Some of our planet's most beautiful scenery is associated with mirror-like bodies of water on a bright sunny day with the scenery of the opposite shore clearly reflected on the water's surface. Water can create mirror-like or specular reflections.

What about white water? Most people have observed white water in waterfalls, rapids in a stream, "whitecaps" on a lake, or perhaps ocean breakers. In those situations where the water surface is anything but smooth, the water is reflecting the light that strikes it, but it is a diffused reflection.

A common example of both types of reflection is the case of a speeding boat on a smooth lake. The lake may be reflecting like a mirror for the most part, but the wake alongside and trailing the boat for a distance is white water. We know that it is the same water and that in both cases the light is being reflected. In this chapter we focus on diffused reflections—the whitewater variety.

The interaction of selective absorption and selective reflection is one of the bases of color. A black object absorbs most of the light that reaches it. A white object reflects most of the light that reaches it. This is, of course, the explanation for why on a hot sunny day a darker car will become hotter while parked in the sun than a lighter colored car.

In the previous chapter we mentioned prisms. We said that some types of prisms reflect most of their light back in the general direction from which the light came. This is the secret of a high-quality diamond used in jewelry. A properly cut high quality diamond loses (absorbs) very little light; it reflects virtually all the light that reaches it. When we say a diamond is "brilliant," it is because of its excellent reflecting ability.

Light is the source of beauty for this planet. In addition to providing life to all on earth, the light from our sun decorates our planet. Color does not belong to an object intrinsically. All flowers are for all practical purposes black! They have no color. This is contrary to common sense—but it is true. This means that the color you see emanating from that beautiful tulip does not belong to it—in fact it was only about eight and one-half minutes ago in the sun! We know color is perceived due to the light which an object reflects.

How is this possible? A yellow object such as a daffodil reflects yellow light. A red sports car reflects red light. Healthy grass reflects green light. A white object reflects all colors and a black object reflects no light.

What happens to the other colors that are not reflected? They are absorbed. As these other colors are absorbed, heat is produced. The darker something looks, the more it is heated by light.

White light can be split into many colors. The light from our sun can be split into literally millions of colors. How many colors are there? Man has names for many thousands of colors; however, there are millions of colors.

How many colors can humans distinguish? Past estimates began near twenty thousand. Today it is believed to be many times more.

One might wonder how man has learned that there are so many colors if we can only distinguish a relatively small percentage of the total number. The process of spectrum analysis allows scientists to look at the various wavelengths of a ray of light. The presence of various wavelengths denotes the corresponding colors. Sophisticated electronic instruments called spectrum analyzers allow the accurate identification of the various wavelengths of light that an object reflects. This process is used by scientists to detect the presence of various substances. It is like the way law enforcement officers use fingerprint detection techniques to detect the past presence of individuals.

The ninety-two naturally occurring chemical elements vary in their construction. Understanding the differences provides the basis for spectrum analysis. These differences and the knowledge that they remain the same for any given element regardless of whether it is found on earth, on a distant star, or in the laboratory, has allowed great advances in man's knowledge.

Spectrum analysis is a valuable tool to modern-day scientists. Through this process astronomers can determine the composition of light rays coming to us from the stars. Knowing the composition of light allows the astronomer to then determine the material properties of the stars.

We are brought back to Einstein's fundamental equation, $E = mc^2$, which says mass (matter) and energy are directly related. We can learn the nature of the material by the composition of the energy.

Fiber optics technology has revolutionized many aspects of man's application of knowledge. One of the areas of biggest change has occurred in the communications industry. How does fiber optics work? It is basically a matter of transmittance and reflection. A rod made of a transparent material allows light to be transmitted (passed through). Light behaves like fluid in a pipe, but light is flowing through solid material. A coating on this "light pipe" causes light to be reflected when it reaches the boundary of the two materials. Light travels down this wire-like transparent strand, ricocheting off the walls (boundaries) of the coated material. It is interesting that usually the coating on the transparent fiber optic material is also a transparent material. The important point, however, is that light passes through the inner material and is reflected or "bounced back" from the coated material.

While on earth Jesus said, "I am the vine, you are the branches" (John 15:5a). Today, if Jesus walked the earth He may well say, "I am the light, you are the fiber."

Application

In this chapter we are considering a reaction to light called reflection. Of interest to us are diffused or irregular reflections.

A good example of irregular reflections is the moon. The moon reflects the sun's light to earth. When we look at the moon, we do not see a clear image of the sun. The moon is a diffused reflector. In our earlier eBook, "*GOD'S NATURE: Sonlight Sunlight*" we saw that just as the moon reflects the sun's light, we as His Church (children of light) should reflect the Son's light. You should be a good reflector of Christ. We should radiate the light of Christ to the dark world all around us.

Another example of diffused reflection is a jewelry-grade diamond. Previously we looked at the analogy of a prism. "If instead of a single prism you could imagine a flawless diamond with dozens or hundreds of facets, then you might get a better idea of God's purposes in you His child. Life here on earth is not solely for the purpose of displaying the Savior, it is also the time during which God adds new facets to His original, flawless diamond—you. God's intention for you and me is not only to manifest His glory in time, but also for eternity. 'There are also heavenly bodies and there are earthly bodies; but the splendor of the heavenly bodies is one kind, and the splendor of the earthly bodies is another. The sun has one kind of splendor, the moon another and the stars another; and star differs from star in splendor. So will it be with the resurrection of the dead. The body that is sown is perishable, it is raised imperishable; it is sown in dishonor, it is raised in glory...' 'Those who are wise will shine like the brightness of the heavens, and those who lead many to righteousness, like the stars for ever and ever' (1 Corinthians 15:40-42 niv; Daniel 12:3 niv). There may be times, extended times, when God as master cutter is adding new facets to our spiritual beings which will be seen only in eternity. Perhaps right now you are being rather painfully faceted. Remember Peter says, 'These (trials) have come so that your faith—of greater worth than gold, which perishes even though refined by fire—may be proved genuine and result in praise, glory and honor when Jesus Christ is revealed' (1 Peter 1:7 niv)."[4] You should be declaring the praises of the One who has called you into His wonderful light. You should be sparkling like a fine diamond, a stark contrast to your surroundings.

Light, as we know, provides the basis to perceive color. We also understand that light is essential to our existence. Light is the basis for sight and the basis for all beauty. Without light this planet would be a black desolate place. We live in a colorful world. I may describe my wife's sweater as blue. She may correct me by calling it turquoise or indigo. I may describe an object as purple, but someone else may say that it is orchid, or mauve, or magenta. We live in a world of azure lakes, emerald lawns, and amber fields of grain. We talk of golden years, brilliant sunsets, and rainbows. We live in a colorful environment, and we think and speak in terms of color.

Just as physical light brings out the beauty of our environment, spiritual light brings out the beauty in human nature. God is light. God is the source of light. The Holy Spirit, a member of the Triune God, produces beauty in the human heart: "But the fruit of the Spirit is love, joy, peace, longsuffering, kindness, goodness, faithfulness, gentleness, self-control" (Galatians 5:22-23).

In the absence of physical light physical objects are black. In the absence of divine light man is in the darkness of spiritual separation from God. Paul in his defense before King Agrippa represented the work which Jesus Christ had commissioned him to do: "to open their eyes, in order to turn them from darkness to light, and from the power of Satan to God" (Acts 26:18).

Light consists of a rainbow of colors. A prism is one method that can easily demonstrate that sunlight is composed of multiple colors. An analogy can also be drawn with respect to color. Different colors may be thought of as the individual talents and gifts that individuals display when the light of God and His Word shines upon them. To one may be given the ability to teach. Another may be gifted in showing love in a practical way to those who are in need. Another person may be gifted musically. Most physical objects reflect many colors, but often one or two colors are predominant. Individuals have many abilities, but usually one or two talents or spiritual gifts will be predominant.

As white is the reflection of all colors, you are to be growing in purity until you are reflecting fully the fruit of the Spirit in all its manifestations. Your nature is to become more and more like Christ's nature.

We may not understand our gifts and talents to the extent that we might like. Again, there may be an analogy in the physical world of color. Science also has a lot of unanswered questions. Jerry was a specialist for a corporation where I was employed. He was a "perceptual physicist" who specialized in color vision. Among the areas of his knowledge were the physics of light, the physiology of vision, and the psychology of perception. Jerry has this to say about our understanding of light: "We really don't know much about light. Theories about electromagnetic waves and quantum mechanics 'work' to some extent, but not well enough for many purposes. Much about the nature of light still eludes modern physics."

Spectrum analysis allows measurement of the various colors an object reflects and the quantity of each. From that data scientists can determine what materials the object is made of. God has His own version of a spectrum analyzer. As He looks at your talents and abilities and the degree to which you are using them, He knows whether, or not, you are living up to your abilities. Luke tells us, "From everyone who has been given much, much will be demanded" (Luke 12:48 niv).

Sunlight / Sonlight

The scientific community uses spectrum analysis to discover the properties of an object.

God uses His own precisely accurate analysis and knows the true properties of a human being and his motivations.

THINK AND GROW

1. Does your life reflect Christ?

2. Do others think of Christ when they think of you?

3. If "1" described pure white water and "10" described a perfectly mirror-like lake surface, where would you rank your present life?

5

Opaque:

Provides No Image

We have looked at the three basic reactions to light. We now come to a group of three chapters which describe material objects. These distinctions are related to how a material reacts to light, that is, how much of the light is absorbed, refracted, and reflected.

An opaque object allows very little or none of the light which reaches it to pass through. Most objects refract, or pass through, some light, but only for a small distance. For example, hold a piece of paper up to a strong light source—some light is passed through. If the opaque material is very thick, it passes no light at all. Since light is not passed through, we will characterize opaque objects as objects which light does not pass through. They allow no image to be seen.

In simple non-scientific terms, materials are characterized in the following way. *Opaque* materials are characterized by *no image, translucent* materials by a *fuzzy image,* and *transparent* materials by a *clear image.*

The sky is a material which can be considered transparent, translucent, or nearly opaque. During a clear day the sky is transparent and sharp shadows are cast; that is, a clear image of an object is given by its shadow. However, the shadow's image is not an accurate one but is incomplete and distorted. When the sky is hazy, it is translucent, and we observe hazy shadows, or shadows which provide a fuzzy image. These shadows are not distinctly defined. Under heavily overcast conditions the sky, while still translucent, may be considered opaque.

Under such conditions there is virtually no shadow and consequently no image.

In addition to these three material responses to light, there is a special reaction to light which is really a category by itself. It is a specialized reaction by any of the three materials, opaque, translucent, or transparent, in which the common thread is that an accurate reproduction of the image is provided. A common mirror is the typical example. We characterize *reproduction* therefore as *providing an accurate image*. Some might object to classifying a mirror as an accurate image since the image is reversed left to right. First, remember that if a second mirror is used, we can indeed gain an exact image. Furthermore, it is important to differentiate an accurate image from the clear image of many transparent materials. Transparent materials often filter out part of the image they transmit. The most common example would be colored glass which filters out some of the color of white light. In such cases there is a clear but incomplete image. The image is clear and distinct, but since only a part of the whole image is transmitted, it is not complete and accurate. In other cases, often caused by the physical shape of a material, transparent materials distort the shape of the image. In this situation the image is deformed rather than accurate. In a later chapter we will look in more detail at this topic.

Opaque

In our surroundings most objects with which we come into contact are opaque. Most of the clothing we wear and the furniture we have are opaque. Opaque objects are in the majority in our homes, buildings, and transportation systems. Opaque objects do not allow light to pass through them. When light strikes an opaque object, part of it is reflected and part is absorbed and becomes heat. The color which we perceive is determined according to which wavelengths of light are reflected and which wavelengths are absorbed.

It is opaque objects that allow us to create darkness where there is light. We have the capability of entering a building under the bright noonday sun, and if there are no windows, we can have total darkness. During my career I once became involved in specifying and building a darkroom for a group of camera engineers. Anyone who has experienced such total darkness for sustained periods will tell you that it is an unnatural environment for human beings. Even the fact that man is so wonderfully equipped for vision should tell us that such darkness is not for man.

When it comes to spiritual darkness, the Word of God tells us that "men loved darkness rather than light, because their deeds were evil" (John 3:19). One night in a Bible study which I led someone quoted that verse. One person quipped, "That's why most taverns don't have any windows!" When you think about it, there's truth in that remark. Usually night clubs and taverns, especially those that were built originally for that purpose, have few if any windows. Furthermore, the lighting is usually very dim. In this case we see a parallel between spiritual darkness and the love of physical darkness.

Another related area is crime. While it is true that more and more burglaries, murders, and other crimes are occurring during daylight, it is also true that most crime is committed at night. Criminals choose to perform their wrongful acts in the darkness of night rather than in broad daylight.

The same is true of spiritual light. Jesus Christ came to earth as the light of the world. Spiritual light is available to all who seek truth, yet many choose to walk in darkness. Listen to the context of the Scripture quoted above: "This is the verdict: Light has come into the world, but men loved darkness instead of light, because their deeds were evil. Everyone who does evil hates the light, and will not come into the light for fear that his deeds will be exposed" (John 3:19-20 niv). When it comes to spiritual light, it is as if there is an opaque shield around man's thinking. Paul put it this way in writing to the Ephesians: "Having their understanding darkened, being alienated from the life of God through the ignorance that is in them, because of the blindness of their heart" (Ephesians 4:18 kjv). Notice Paul's use of the words "darkened" and "blindness." The word "alienated" suggests separation from the true light, like having an opaque screen between!

Application

There are several observations concerning opaque objects. First, opaque objects transmit no light—they allow no light to pass through. Because no light passes through opaque objects, they create shadows. Additionally, surrounding a space with opaque objects will create total darkness within that space. As a child of light your manner of life should be such that others see God in you, the God who is light. The light of God should change you. You should not appear like the majority around you. If you claim to know God but do not allow His light to pass through you, you are causing a shadow. You are decreasing the available light to others.

Second, we noticed that most physical objects in our environment are opaque. We observed that opaque objects reflect and absorb light. We also know that heat will be generated in proportion to the amount of light that is absorbed. Just as physical light is bounced off, that is reflected off most physical objects, so also the Word of God makes it plain that most individuals have allowed the spiritual light of God to bounce off them, with only a relatively small amount absorbed. Just as physical opaque objects absorb some of the light which reaches them, human beings absorb some of the spiritual light available to them. Just as physical objects absorb different portions of physical light, individuals absorb different parts of the truth of God.

For example, it is a rare opaque object that is a true white, absorbing virtually no physical light whatever. It is also rare to find an individual so spiritually opaque as to have absorbed none of the truth of Christianity. Consider the following example.

As light is soaked up or absorbed, heat is generated. An individual may have absorbed the Scripture that says, "God is love," and it may provide some warmth. (It would provide greater heat if the truth of God's wrath and justice were fully comprehended.) Later that same person may come to believe at least intellectually that Jesus Christ is who He claimed to be—the Son of God and the light of the world. Still later, our example individual may come to believe that Jesus Christ did in fact die on Calvary's Cross for the sins of the world. However, it is not until our friend in the example comes to realize, understand, fully absorb, and act upon the reality that Jesus Christ died for his personal sins that it has a significant effect.

The more physical light is absorbed, the darker the object becomes. In human pride and human self-righteousness, we tend to see ourselves as being all right, as white objects. But as in the above example, as spiritual light is absorbed, we begin to see ourselves in darker colors. The more spiritual light is soaked up, the blacker we see ourselves. As we accept the entire light spectrum of the essentials of Christianity, we view ourselves in blackness of sin and the darkness of spiritual poverty and blindness. The Word of God says that as we become willing to admit the truth of our condition and acknowledge our need of the Savior, we become new creatures. It is as if we are changed from the blackness of coal to the brilliance of a diamond. Both are primarily carbon, but what a difference! A diamond is a new or different creation from coal. The spiritual light and life which is found only in Jesus Christ makes as startling a difference as the difference between coal and a diamond. The apostle Paul stated it this way: "Therefore, if anyone is in Christ, he is a new creation; old things have passed away; behold, all things have become new" (2 Corinthians 5:17).

Sunlight / Sonlight

Opaque objects provide no image of the light source which strikes them. When sunlight strikes an opaque object no light is passed through.

Opaque individuals provide no image of the Sonlight as it shines on them. When Sonlight strikes such an individual none is passed through.

THINK AND GROW

1. Which do you love more, light or darkness?

2. Does your life most resemble a chunk of coal or a beautifully faceted diamond?

6

Translucent:
Provides a Fuzzy Image

In the previous chapter we considered opaque materials, characterized by reflecting and absorbing some of the light, but not transmitting or passing through any light. We observed that since *opaque* materials do not pass any light through, they provide *no image*.

We come now to translucent materials. When light strikes a translucent material, part of the light is reflected and part of it is absorbed, as in opaque materials, but some of it is also passed through or transmitted. An important consideration with *translucent* material is that the light which is passed through is scattered or diffused, resulting in a *fuzzy*, diffused image.

Often the image will be so fuzzy that the word image might be questionable. However, if a light source is placed behind an opaque object such as a building wall, it is not detectable. On the other hand, if a light source is placed behind a translucent object such as a patterned bathroom window, it is very detectable. In this case it is evidence of a light source on the other side, but we cannot see what it is. If a person or other object moves near the window in such a way that it is between the light source and the translucent window, a fuzzy image in the form of a shadow might be observed from the other side. In another common example, in many glass shower doors the image of a person may be seen, particularly if the shower is well lighted, but the image will lack definition—it will be a fuzzy image.

In the next chapter we will consider transparent materials. In order to keep these three types of materials separate in our thinking, the common light bulb may be used as an example. Most of the light bulbs which are purchased are "frosted" bulbs. These have translucent glass envelopes or bulbs that surround the filament or lighting source. When one of these bulbs glow, the filament is a fuzzy image inside. With the electricity off, a fuzzy image of the filament can be seen by holding the bulb up to a strong light source. Fluorescent light tubes are also normally translucent.

There are also clear light bulbs that are used for special purposes such as flashlights and automobile lights. Clear bulbs are also often used for special effect lighting such as behind cut glass enclosures or in dining room fixtures. These transparent bulbs provide a clear image of the filament—regardless of whether the electricity is on or off. The brilliance of a point source of light is desired for some applications as compared to the larger diffused glow of a frosted bulb.

Our final example of light bulbs is a little less common. In previous years many high-wattage incandescent light bulbs that were used in large rooms were painted with a thick silver paint on the end away from the screw-in socket. This bulb was designed to be mounted with the painted surface down. It was a highly reflective opaque paint that reflected light back into the bulb so that essentially all the light came out of the upper portion of the bulb. This caused diffused, indirect lighting as the light was reflected off the ceiling or a reflector that was part of the fixture.

My wife Connie loves candles, and I must admit that I enjoy them also. Years ago, we were given a beautiful white wax candle about four inches in diameter which had two butterflies mounted inside near the surface of the wax. They were of different species, and each was very colorful. The candle was very pretty, but it was not until it was lit and the flame had burned down into the candle some distance, giving a glow to the entire candle, that the true beauty was seen.

On another occasion we were given a candle with myrtle wood shavings embedded in the wax near the surface. Again, the beauty of the candle was significantly increased as the flame allowed greater beauty of the wood grain and texture to be seen. Candles of this type are made of translucent wax. The candle flame inside the translucent material is seen as a fuzzy image. The flame lights up the entire candle. The entire candle has a glow.

In our discussion of opaque objects we said that some light will pass through a thin opaque object. The example given was a thin piece of paper held up to a strong light. In that case paper is translucent. Now we find that under certain conditions a translucent material which normally provides a fuzzy image may provide a clear image, so that it has the effect of a transparent material. This is commonly seen in candles where a thin layer of translucent wax is covering the object and the light of the flame backlights the object. The butterflies and the wood chips were deliberately placed by the candle maker close to the outside of the candle. The result was that the translucent material simultaneously gave a clear image of the butterflies and a fuzzy image of the flame. The candle was transparent with respect to the butterflies but translucent with respect to the flame. The reason for the two conditions is the thickness of the material.

The concept of an opaque object sometimes appearing transparent and a translucent object sometimes appearing transparent are further examples of how the concepts we are considering in this chapter are intricately woven together. It is difficult to look at one aspect of interaction with light by itself without considering other aspects.

There are many common examples of translucent materials. Automobile taillights are usually made of translucent material. If the taillight was transparent, you would see a very bright spot in the taillight where the filament of the light bulb was burning, and the remainder of the taillight would be relatively dim. Vehicle taillights typically are translucent and it is difficult to determine precisely where the filament is located.

Mankind has learned to use translucent materials well. Since translucent materials scatter or diffuse light, there are many very practical uses for them. The automobile taillight, the bathroom window, the shower door, and the frosted light bulb are all examples. Many lamp shades are made of translucent material in order to diffuse or soften the light. (Some lamp shades are opaque or even transparent.) Likewise, most fluorescent light fixtures use a diffuser of some type. Many times, such as fluorescent fixtures for residential use, the diffuser is a piece of translucent material placed between the light bulb and the direction it is intended to illuminate.

Translucent materials are often used in advertising. Many business signs are made of a translucent plastic material. Marquee billboard type signs such as those theaters and supermarkets use to put colored letters on are made of a translucent material.

In recent weeks our area experienced a severe windstorm. Many trees were uprooted or even broken off. Significant damage occurred to many homes and businesses. Many of this type of signs had their diffusion panels broken. Now a clear image of what caused the signs to glow could be observed. I could count the number of individual fluorescent tubes and observe their placement. Previously only the glow of light which lit up the sign could be observed.

Application

Translucent materials reflect, absorb, and transmit light. Most of the light which is passed through translucent materials is scattered or diffused. We receive a fuzzy image rather than a clear image. Translucent material may appear as transparent material under certain conditions. The candle examples were given in illustration. It is also quite common for translucent materials to appear almost opaque. Consider the wax candle when it is not burning, or the advertising sign during bright sunlight hours.

When translucent materials have a strong light source on the opposite side of them from the observer, they have a glow which makes them distinct from either opaque or transparent materials.

Again, there are analogies between physical light and spiritual light. The sun "radiates" energy to us in the form of sunlight. We sometimes speak of a "radiant" person. As a Christian you should radiate the Son to those around you.

At one time or another we have all seen light in a person's face. As a Christian, as a child of light, you are not called upon to put light in people's faces, but to point people towards the One who can put a permanent light within their countenance.

In earlier chapters we saw how God is light and how He sent His Son Jesus Christ into the world as the light of the world. "For it is the God who commanded light to shine out of darkness, who has shone in our hearts to give the light of the knowledge of the glory of God in the face of Jesus Christ" (2 Corinthians 4:6).

The Old Testament also contains this theme of light: "The path of the righteous is like the first gleam of dawn, shining ever brighter till the full light of day" (Proverbs 4:18 niv).

As a child of God, that is a child of light, you are now also called upon to be a light in this dark world. In his letter to the Philippians Paul tells us, "For it is God who works in you... that you may become blameless and harmless, children of God without fault in the midst of a crooked and perverse generation, among whom you shine as lights in the world" (Philippians 2:13, 15).

As a child of light you should have a glow about you that radiates out to those around you. Matthew wrote, "Let your light so shine before men, that they may see your good works and glorify your Father in heaven" (Matthew 5:16).

The purpose of light is to dispel darkness. The brighter or more intense the light, the greater its effect can be. Intensity is dependent upon the amount of power. Power is dependent upon walking in the light. John wrote: "But if we walk in the light *as He is in the light*, we have fellowship with one another, and the blood of Jesus Christ His Son cleanses us from all sin" (1 John 1:7).

In this verse there is a significant change in what John has written. In 1 John 1:5 it says, "God is light," but now in verse seven we read that God is *in* the light. It is as if John is saying that God is fully revealed and able to be seen. Recall that we said that light is self-manifesting. This is true of both physical and spiritual light. When John says God is *in* the light, it seems that he is telling us that God has fully revealed Himself to us—that we can see God! Jesus while on earth spoke to Philip: "Don't you know me, Philip, even after I have been among you such a long time? Anyone who has seen Me has seen the Father. How can you say, 'Show us the Father?'" (John 14:9 niv). When Jesus Christ came to earth as the light of the world, God was revealed and made manifest to mankind.

This same verse (1 John 1:7) says "if *we* walk *in* the light." This is not the same thing as walking according to the light, but *in* the light. In other words, your walk is before the eyes of God, enlightened by the full revelation of who He is. It is not that there is no sin in you, as the rest of 1 John 1 makes so clear. The expression "walking in the light" refers to a fact! It is not a reference to the degree to which the ideal has been realized.

With these thoughts in mind the verse has added meaning. "But if we walk in the light as He is in the light, we have fellowship with one another, and the blood of Jesus Christ His Son cleanses us from all sin" (1 John 1:7). This verse holds three essentials to your position as a child of light; walking in the light as God is in it, having fellowship with other children of light, and cleansing from all sin by the blood of Christ at Calvary's Cross. Walking in His light, fellowshipping with other children of light, and having no unconfessed sin in your life (see verses 9-10) will allow you to increase the intensity of your light.

Are you making the world brighter?

We noted in this chapter that translucent materials sometimes appear almost opaque, that is there is little evidence of light being transmitted. If the translucent material is examined closely, it does have a slightly different appearance than true opaque objects. The translucent wax candle without a flame has a different appearance than the wood table on which it is setting, or even than a wax candle made of opaque wax. The automobile taillight that is off appears different than the chrome bezel or painted trunk lid, or the opaque materials used in the car's interior. But given a strong light source and the observer in the right location with respect to translucent material, that which appeared almost opaque now takes on a new foreign radiance.

An analogy is seen here also. A child of light may not be walking in the light, fellowshipping, and confessing sin. Such a one will not have the radiance of Christ but when examined closely there is still something different from those around. But when that one allows the true light to shine into his being and begins again to walk *in* the light, a radiance becomes observable.

Sunlight / Sonlight

Translucent objects transmit a fuzzy image of sunlight.

Individuals sometimes transmit a fuzzy image of Sonlight.

THINK AND GROW

1. Are you making the world brighter?

2. Is there a discernible glow about your life?

7

Transparent:
Provides a Clear Image

We come now to the third material description. We remember that opaque objects absorb and reflect light but do not allow light to pass through. *Opaque* materials allow us to see *no image* of what is on the opposite side.

Translucent materials, in addition to absorbing and reflecting light, also allow light to pass through. The characteristic of translucent materials, however, is that the light which is passed through is diffused or scattered so that a clear image is not seen. *Translucent* materials are those which provide a *fuzzy* image of what is on the opposite side.

In this chapter we consider the third and final type of materials, those which are transparent. These materials absorb and reflect light as do opaque and translucent materials. Transparent materials also allow light to pass through as do translucent materials. When light passes through transparent material, the individual light rays move in a uniform predictable direction, in contrast to the scattering which occurs in translucent material. The characteristic of *transparent* materials is that they provide a *clear image* of what is on the opposite side. The glass window is a common example of transparent material.

Light, as we have seen, is revealing. In darkness nothing is revealed to our vision. To discover what is in a totally dark room requires the use of hearing, smelling, or tactile senses, followed by a mental process which allows us to form conclusions about the room's contents. But if light enters the room, the contents of the room are revealed because of the process which we call vision.

There is a story which has been told many times, with which I suspect most of us can identify. A young girl was sweeping and sweeping an old wooden cottage. It seemed that she wasn't making much headway. The bright sunshine was streaming through the window and it seemed as if she was only stirring up the dust so that it would settle in new locations. Finally, in exasperation she emotionally moved briskly to the window and yanked down the shade. Her mother, rocking quietly in a corner of the cottage, asked her why she had acted so. Her reply: "The sun makes the room so dusty."

Now we know, and I expect that young girl knew, that the sun doesn't *make* anything dusty. But the light does reveal what is already there. It reminds us again of the wisdom of John's words, "men loved darkness rather than light, because their deeds were evil" (John 3:19). If man's deeds were righteous, he would not mind the spiritual light, just as the young girl would not mind the bright sunlight if the cabin was without dust and dirt.

When a person is guilty, he is never at ease with one who accuses him. This is true not only in our relationships with one another but also in mankind's relationship with the Creator. A sinful person seeks to hide from a holy and righteous God. We see this in the first recorded sin. Adam tried to hide from God after he sinned, and notice that he said, "I was afraid because I was naked; and I hid" (Genesis 3:10). Adam realized that he was transparent before an all-knowing God, so he hid himself. Knowing he was visible, Adam sought to make himself opaque to God.

The apostle Luke recorded Jesus' words: "For there is nothing covered that will not be revealed, nor hidden that will not be known. Therefore whatever you have spoken in the dark will be heard in the light, and what you have spoken in the ear in inner rooms will be proclaimed on the housetops" (Luke 12:2-3). Since mankind is transparent before

God, it seems obvious that we need a satisfactory relationship with God. Jesus Christ, the Light of the World, has provided us the opportunity for a correct and good relationship with God, who is light. We have the opportunity of becoming children of light.

Peter tells of a new relationship and purpose as children of light. "But you are a chosen generation, a royal priesthood, a holy nation, His own special people, *that you may proclaim the praises of Him who called you out of darkness into His marvelous light*" (1 Peter 2:9).

Transparent materials have allowed the invention of many interesting devices. Windows and prisms have previously been mentioned. When man learned to make lenses, it allowed the development of magnifiers, microscopes, telescopes, and cameras. The study of optics and optical systems is a complex field that has seen significant strides in recent years, largely due to the use of computers in lens design. Fiber optics has been previously mentioned as a new field of technology that is based largely upon the use of transparent materials.

In many of the typical examples of transparent materials it is very easy to think in terms of high quality *clear* transparent materials, but it is important to remember that many transparent materials are not clear. High quality transparent *filters* are used in many optical applications. For instance, colored filters and polarizing filters are commonly used in photography and other optical work. Although many applications of filters are for technical uses, some are for artistic purposes. Mankind has probably never used filters for any more beauty and grandeur than in stained glass windows in his places of worship. (Many of these pieces of glass are translucent colored filters rather than transparent.)

We take so much for granted. Even the clarity of our common window glass would have been a real marvel a few centuries ago. "Glass has been manufactured for some five thousand years, but for many thousand years no one knew how to make uncolored glass, something which you did not look *at,* but *through:* you always saw through a glass darkly."[5] Notice this description of early glass being something you looked "at." Glass was a colored, "translucent" material which provided only a fuzzy image at best. Remember Paul's illustration to the Corinthian church, "For now we see through a glass darkly; but then face to face: now I know in part; but then shall I know even as also I am known" (1 Corinthians 13:12 kjv). Most Bible scholars believe that the word "glass" means mirror in this passage. If this interpretation is right, then the meaning is doubly clear since light passes through glass to the mirrored surface and then back through the glass to the observer. This verse is translated in the New International Version as follows, "Now we see but a poor reflection; then we shall see face to face. Now I know in part; then I shall know fully, even as I am fully known" (1 Corinthians 13:12, niv).

But what effect does colored glass have on light? Any colored transparent material is a filter. It filters or removes some of the light. In the case of colored transparent material it removes some of the wavelengths of light, coloring the image that is seen. The white light image that enters a transparent piece of amber glass is viewed on the opposite side as a clearly defined but amber colored image.

Polarization filters are often used in optical work. A polarizing filter filters out wavelengths of light that are oriented in a specific direction. Many people wear polarized sunglasses. These glasses have polarized filters to block the reflected glare that comes to a person who is in an upright position. Next time you wear polarized glasses on a bright day, try leaning your head as far down toward your shoulder as possible. Next slowly raise your head and continue to your opposite shoulder. The effectiveness of the sunglasses, *in the upright vertical position,* will be very apparent.

Previously we observed that in order to explain light's behavior satisfactorily, scientists use a dualistic approach. Many times light must be considered as particles with straight-line motion. Other times light must be thought of as a waveform. In polarization, light is considered under the wave theory. In order to avoid technical detail about polarization, we will think of polarized light by use of a simplified illustration. If someone places a polarizing filter in front of a camera lens, it will block those light waves that are moving in a specific orientation. For this example, we will assume that the filter absorbs all light waves that are closer to a true horizontal position than to a true vertical position. Polarizing lenses usually have a provision for rotation in order to change the effect on the film. If therefore this polarizing filter is rotated ninety degrees, it will block the passage of, or filter, all light waves with a vertical orientation, while allowing the horizontal light waves to pass through. If we now install a second polarizing filter so that one is positioned to block horizontal light and the other is positioned to stop vertical rays, no light will pass through and into the camera lens.

Application

Are there spiritual analogies regarding transparent materials? First, as a child of light you should seek to "pass through" the full light of God to others around you. To do this you must be transparent. Sin in the life causes a hiding from God. Your natural tendency, that is your Adamic tendency, is to seek to be opaque, to put up a veneer, and to not be transparent to God or to others. You hide your failures and you hide your needs. You tend to hide your true self from others, and you try to fool yourself into thinking you can be opaque to God. You find that it is quite traumatic to allow others to see you as you really are. You need to learn with God's help how to live your life so that you do not have to fear openness and transparency. As a "child of light" you should live a transparent life and expose yourself to God's will.

We previously considered the light of the world and saw that the Church as a united whole is a light unto this dark and needy world. The Church needs to be careful not to filter out part of the true light.

Filters transmit a true and clear image, but not a complete and accurate image. If as a Church we preach about the virgin birth of Christ, His sinless life, His death, burial, and resurrection, but fail to preach about the purpose and meaning of His death, we are filtering. If we proclaim the love of God, His goodness, His mercy, and His grace, we have a responsibility to also proclaim His purity and holiness, which results in His wrath and hatred of sin. If we do not proclaim the whole truth, we are like a colored filter.

There is a device called a *beam splitter* that is used in optical laboratories. A beam splitter does exactly what its name implies; it splits a light beam and sends a portion of the light in a new direction while the remainder of the light continues in its original path. Many years ago I became directly involved in an engineering project utilizing two lasers with ten beam splitters for each laser. One of the significant results of a beam splitter is the reduction in intensity of the light. In this project each area received only about ten percent of the laser's light. If we proclaim the whole truth of Christianity but water it down, we are reacting like a beam splitter.

Polarization filters are also possible within the Church. If we teach man's responsibility to man, the horizontal dimension of Christianity, without teaching the need for a vertical personal relationship with God, the vertical dimension of Christianity, we are utilizing a polarization filter. The opposite situation is nothing more than a rotation of the polarizer. If two of these polarizers are used, one each for our manward and Godward responsibilities, no light comes through at all.

Lenses and optics also provide parallels. Optics allow us to focus light rays in useful ways. A magnifier will cause something to appear larger, a most useful device. Lenses such as magnifiers can also be used to focus the light at a single point. Previously I recalled how my daughter had focused the sunlight on a piece of wood. The intensity of the sunlight was increased at a chosen spot, causing so much heat that the wood burst into flame. Prayer seems to me to be somewhat analogous to a focusing lens. Through prayer we seek to focus the love of God, the power of God, the fullness of God on a specific item. The light and power will be focused on a specific task.

At other times prayer may be thought of as a window. In prayer you lift the shade from the window and spiritual light flows in. Light floods in like the water from a dam that has broken. The light touches, illuminates, brightens, and transforms even the darkest spots. The whole aspect of the room, or of your life, is changed.

One final thing about transparent materials—they do not produce shadows. Transparent materials do not hide the light from others. That light which transparent material receives is to a significant extent passed along to others.

Sunlight / Sonlight

Sunlight passes through transparent materials in a way that provides an image on the other side of the material from the light source.

Sonlight passes through some individuals in a way that provides an image of Sonlight.

THINK AND GROW

1. Are you transmitting Sonlight to others?

2. If so, is it a clear (uncolored) image?

8

Summary:

Opaque, Translucent & Transparent

There are three basic types of materials regarding their reactions to light. Opaque materials provide "no image," translucent materials provide only a "fuzzy image," and transparent materials provide a "clear image," although not necessarily a complete image.

The three materials may be thought of in another way. Consider an individual who is surrounded by one of these materials. In the case of the opaque material there is no change in the individual's condition or environment when a strong light source is beamed at the enclosure. It is just as dark inside the enclosure after the light source is aimed as it was before.

If the material is changed to a translucent material and a light source is directed at the enclosure, the environment is changed. The inside of the enclosure is illuminated as the entire enclosure is aglow. The individual senses a dramatic change but cannot clearly see what it is that has changed the material.

If now there is transparent material surrounding the person, the environment is illuminated, and the light source is clearly seen.

As a child of light you need to examine your life to see if it exhibits no change, a radiance, or illumination with a clear definition of the source that has caused the change. Does Jesus Christ, the Light of the World, shine brighter in this dark world because of you? Are you opaque, translucent, or transparent? Do you transmit clearly, transmit vaguely, or obscure His pure light?

In the physical world objects can change. Water can change to fog or to ice and back again. Carbon is the primary substance of both lowly coal (opaque) and exalted diamonds (transparent). Sometimes your life is not consistent. You may shine as a diamond in a group of fellow children of light and then take on the appearance of opaque coal with the folks at the office.

In the physical world all three classes of material absorb some of the light that reaches them. Absorption produces heat. Since light is energy, there is a necessary association of light and heat. In the spiritual realm many of us have a snare which retards us. We rejoice in the light but we resist admitting the accompanying heat into our innermost beings. One of the common ways in which we do this is by pursuing more knowledge of the truth without pursuing the knowledge of Him, the Lord Jesus Christ, who is the Truth. The result becomes a spiritual pride which is the worst form of all pride.

The Parable of the Sower

Jesus Christ told a parable about the sowing of seed. "At about that same time Jesus left the house and sat on the beach. In no time at all a crowd gathered along the shoreline, forcing Him to get into a boat. Using the boat as a pulpit, He addressed his congregation, telling stories. 'What do you make of this? A farmer planted seed. As he scattered the seed, some of it fell on the road, and birds ate it. Some fell in the gravel; it sprouted quickly but didn't put down roots, so when the sun came up it withered just as quickly. Some fell in the weeds; as it came up, it was strangled by the weeds. Some fell on good earth, and produced a harvest beyond his wildest dreams. Are you listening to this? Really listening?'" (Matthew 13:1-9 The Message.)

In the parable we have four descriptions of what happens to seed. The results are easily separated into three categories. First, we have seed that falls on a hard surface and therefore *does not take root*. This can be compared to light falling on an opaque object where no light is absorbed.

The next two situations, seed falling on hard-packed ground and seed being choked out by weeds, the seeds only develop *shallow roots* and can be likened to light falling on translucent materials where only some of the light is absorbed. Liken the hard ground to those humans today who respond to a "health and wealth" presentation and come to Christ for "what's in it for me?" When their life hits new bumps they move on to the next potential solution to life's problems. Compare the seed which is choked out by weeds to those who make a confession for Christ but never really make Jesus Christ the Lord of their lives. Pressures of daily living with its many cares and their "love of the world" choke out the claim of Christ on their lives.

Finally, there is the seed falling on good ground and producing *deep roots* like light falling on transparent materials. The seed is sown, watered, and a seedling develops which over time develops into a mature plant.

With this analogy consider how it fits with the interpretation of the parable which we find later in the same chapter of Scripture. "Study this story of the farmer planting seed. When anyone hears news of the kingdom and doesn't take it in, it just remains on the surface, and so the Evil One comes along and plucks it right out of that person's heart. This is the seed the farmer scatters on the road. The seed cast in the gravel — this is the person who hears and instantly responds with enthusiasm. But there is no soil of character, and so when the emotions wear off and some difficulty arrives, there is nothing to show for it. The seed cast in the weeds is the person who hears the kingdom news, but weeds of worry and illusions about getting more and wanting everything under the sun strangle what was heard, and nothing comes of it. The seed cast on good earth is the person who hears and takes in the News, and then produces a harvest beyond his wildest dreams" (Matthew 13:18-23 The Message).

Sunlight / Sonlight

Three basic reactions of physical materials to sunlight allow no image to be seen, a fuzzy image, or a clear image.

Three basic reactions of humans to Sonlight allow no image to be seen, a fuzzy image, or a clear image.

THINK AND GROW

1. Are you willing to accept the heat which comes with the light?

2. How would you characterize your soil? Are you impervious to the penetration of Sonlight? Are you like hard-packed ground or is your life full of weeds? Or, are you maturing as you bask in Sonlight?

2. What kind of image of Sonlight do others see when they look at you? No image? A fuzzy image? A clear image?

9

Reproduction:
Provides an Accurate Image

We have considered opaque materials which provide *no image,* translucent materials which provide a *fuzzy image,* and transparent materials which provide a *clear image.* In this chapter we will look at reproduction, which is characterized by a complete and *accurate image.* An accurate image may be reproduced by any of the three types of materials.

The antithesis of an accurate image is an inaccurate or distorted image. In the next three chapters we will consider images which are inaccurate due to *distorted color* ("substitutes"), *distorted image* ("mirages"), and *distorted intensity* ("shadows"). The astute reader may recognize a parallelism between these three descriptions and what has been said in the preceding three chapters.

At the outset of our discussion dealing with interactions to light, we saw that all the chapters are interrelated in various complex ways. As we now consider reproduction, we find that there are three primary ways to obtain an accurate image. They all relate to *reflection,* and they all have a mirror-like aspect to them. A silversmith was asked, "How do you know when the silver is pure?" He replied, "When I see my reflection in it."

An Accurate Image

An accurate image may be obtained by reflection on a polished *opaque* object. Often we will notice such a reflection on a highly waxed and polished automobile. It is particularly noticeable on a black or other dark-colored auto. However, in the case of an automobile it is rare to find a flat enough surface to provide an undistorted image. Many uncoated metals are capable of being polished to such a degree as to provide a mirror-like surface. A highly polished metal surface which is then plated with a metal such as chromium can provide an extremely reflective surface.

The second way to obtain an accurate image is very similar to the first. A very smooth or highly polished surface on a *translucent* object will also produce an accurate image by the reaction called reflection.

The third way is also similar. Reflections from a *transparent* material can provide an accurate image. A typical way this may be observed is by approaching from the side a large plate glass window. Reflections are more likely to be pronounced if the window is in the shade and there are some objects in full sunlight across from the window—in which case the window acts like a mirror. Probably everyone has at one time or another noticed the mirror-like qualities of an ordinary clear window.

We accept high quality reflections with little thought during our everyday living. We are so accustomed to getting up in the morning and looking into our bathroom mirrors that we rarely give them a second thought. In our automobiles we have mirrors that are very functional. Some mirrors are used strictly for decor in our homes and offices. Modern architecture often makes use of highly reflective surfaces of glass and other materials on tall buildings in order to provide a changing panorama which harmonizes with the color of the sky and the cloud formations. We accept highly reflective surfaces as a standard component of our environment.

Have you ever watched a young child amusing himself with a mirror for the first time? Or how about a kitten or other pet? Mirrors are intriguing if they are not commonplace. Primitive people have always regarded mirrors as a simply delightful gift. When a mirror is first given to such a person, there is an immediate infatuation and wonder with the marvelous object that allows one to see oneself. Usually after a few minutes or so, another delightful realization will be made. By adjusting the angle of the mirror, you can see your feet, or what is above you, or even what is behind you without moving your head.

What is it that is so intriguing about a mirror-surface? Is it not that we are able to see ourselves instead of the object at which we are looking at, that we can see the tree that is behind us while we are looking straight ahead? The great wonder of a mirror is that *while we are looking at one object, we can see another.*

Application

When others look at you, they should not see you but Christ. Just as Christ is the image of His Father, you as a child of light should take on the family resemblance so that your image becomes more and more like Jesus Christ. Colossians 1:15, concerning Jesus Christ, says that "He is the image of the invisible God." And Paul wrote concerning the children of light: "But we all, with unveiled face beholding as in a mirror the glory of the Lord, are being transformed into the same image from glory to glory" (2 Corinthians 3:18 nasb).

In the Old Testament the glory of God (God light) filled the tabernacle. Today the Spirit of God (God light) lives within the children of light—those who are the temple of the Holy Spirit.

As a child of the light you should ask yourself whether you are reflecting the image of Christ. To an affirmative answer comes the follow-up question: are you reflecting His image accurately, or is it distorted, something more like a funhouse / arcade mirror?

The light of the world, Jesus Christ, needs to be reflected towards those who are in darkness around you. "For it is the God who commanded light to shine out of darkness, who has shone in our hearts to give the light of the knowledge of the glory of God in the face of Jesus Christ" (2 Corinthians 4:6).

As others look at you, do they only see themselves, as if in a mirror, or are you focused upon Christ in such a way that you are reflecting His image to those around you? What a tragedy if others viewing you only see themselves. It is not enough to be capable of producing an accurate image, you are to be positioned in such a way as to produce the *right* accurate image. You must be producing a Christ-like image rather than reflecting the image of your observers.

How do we make sure that we reflect the right image? In 2 Corinthians 3:18 (niv), we read: "And we, who with unveiled faces all reflect the Lord's glory, are being transformed into His likeness with ever-increasing glory, which comes from the Lord, who is the Spirit." Two things stand out as clues. First, you are to be with unveiled, or unfiltered faces. You must accept the whole truth without filters, beam splitters, or polarizers. Second, Paul wrote that you "are being transformed." It is present tense, an ongoing process; you must not expect instant spiritual maturity. The Scripture does not teach immediate spiritual completeness.

In order to be sure that you are not filtering the truth, you must do two things. First, you must study the entire truth. One absolutely vital aspect of this is to become familiar with the whole Word of God. Second, you must apply the Word of God to your daily life. We read, "Do not merely listen to the Word, and so deceive yourselves. Do what it says. Anyone who listens to the Word but does not do what it says is like a man who looks at his face in a mirror and, after looking at himself, goes away and immediately forgets what he looks like. But the man who looks intently into the perfect law that gives freedom, and continues to do this, not forgetting what he has heard, but doing it—he will be blessed in what he does" (James 1:22-25 niv). In these verses the Scriptures present the analogy of the Bible being like a mirror. The light is God, for "God is light." His written Word, the Holy Bible, is the mirror that allows you to see yourself as you really are.

It is possible to produce an "accurate image" not only by the process of reflection but also by transmitting the image through a suitable piece of transparent material. No one will ever attain spiritual perfection in this life, except the One who is perfect—Jesus Christ. However, you should live in such a way as to be gaining in victory over sin and thereby have an openness and transparency of life which is in marked contrast to those around. 2 Peter 1:4 niv says that you are to "participate in the divine nature." You should be taking on the nature of Christ. Your image is to be transformed more and more like unto the image of Christ. Mark Twain once wrote: "Few things are as hard to put up with as the annoyance of a good example." What the world needs are good role models. "That you may become blameless and harmless, children of God without fault in the midst of a crooked and perverse generation, *among whom you shine as lights in the world*" (Philippians 2:15).

As you shine for Christ, it may be well to consider the effects of dark adaptation. Coming out of a dark room into bright sunlight is discomforting. Similarly, sitting in a dark room and having brilliant lights come on instantly is very abrupt. This is why some buildings have lights which are raised gradually so that vision can adjust at a comfortable rate. It seems clear that God took this into account when He created the universe and the sunrise which we experience each day. In many cases, we should keep this principle in mind when you seek to win others to Jesus Christ.

There is another analogy of reproduction. Through the process of photography, we can produce some very accurate images. Prior to the digital revolution in photography a popular film format was 35 mm.

Most film used in these cameras was color slide film or positive transparency film.

Color slide film starts out as a very transparent piece of plastic of uniform thickness. Since it comes in a roll, cameras are carefully designed to hold the film flat at the time of exposure. As the film is produced, it is coated with an "emulsion," a dark opaque mixture of chemicals. In the camera the film is advanced a section at a time in order to line up with the lens of the camera. At the instant a picture is taken the shutter opens, allowing light to enter through the lens into the camera, exposing the film.

From the time light reaches the film, the film is changed completely. The film now has a latent image that is not discernible by the casual observer. It now requires processing to bring the image out into its full color and beauty. When that processing is complete, the film will be a beautiful transparent material which is an accurate image of that on which it was focused at the time of exposure. The film was unattractive, but now that it has become what it was created for, it is full of beauty.

In many ways the photographic process is analogous to the child of light. We know that Adam was a transparent individual before a Holy God. But when sin came into Adam's life, he became very opaque. Furthermore, the process affected all of humanity.

Now through the process of rebirth, individual frames on the film may be instantly changed through exposure to spiritual light. The child of light now has the latent image of light but requires further processing in order to bring out the beauty and the detail of the image of Christ. The child of God is changed from a lost sinner to a child of light. Because of the change that has taken place, the child of light can have true fellowship with other children of light and even with God Himself. "That you also may have fellowship with us; and truly our fellowship is with the Father and with His Son Jesus Christ" (1 John 1:3).

~ *Quote* ~ "Ministers should be stars to give light, not clouds to obscure." —Charles H. Spurgeon

Sunlight / Sonlight

An accurate image can be made when sunlight is reflected off opaque, translucent, or transparent materials.

An accurate image of Sonlight can be reflected when one becomes a child of light, studies the Word of God, and applies it to his life.

THINK AND GROW

1. Have you, like photographic film, become what you were created for?

2. When someone looks at you, do they see themselves, or do they see the Son of God?

10

Substitutes:

Distorted Color

Mankind has labeled sunlight as "white light." Other lights are measured against the sun. The "color temperature" of light is basically the difference in proportion of various light wavelengths (color) as compared to sunlight. Mankind has been able to make artificial suns.

In the spiritual realm all light should be measured against the standard of Sonlight. "In the same way, let your light shine before men, that they may see your good deeds and praise your Father in heaven" (Matthew 5:16 niv).

In our daily lives artificial or substitute lighting has become so commonplace we have learned to take it for granted. Modern man moves around almost as freely at night as during the day. Our homes have traditionally been lit largely by incandescent lighting. Offices are generally lighted with fluorescent lighting. Up until the early seventies most of our streets were lighted with mercury-vapor lamps. Then a substantial portion of our highways and roadways utilized the more energy-efficient sodium lighting before moving on to even more energy-efficient artificial lighting. Cameras took pictures in dim light situations with the aid of flashbulbs. Now this has changed to electronic flash units—usually built into the camera. Our automobiles and other vehicles produce their own electricity so that we may continue to be highly mobile during the hours of darkness. With the aid of artificial light we entertain ourselves with movies and television. Sporting events of all kinds use vast quantities of energy in order to provide entertainment to an increasingly spectator society. Artificial lighting is also used for some participant sports such as night golfing and night skiing.

Although a portion of our lighting is for recreational and convenience purposes, it is also true that a substantial portion of artificial lighting is primarily protective in nature. Street lighting is not only for convenience and the safety that is derived from improved vision, but also largely for protection from other members of our society. In primitive times our ancestors recognized the safety of sunlight. Before darkness came, they returned to caves and crude huts for protection from the uncertainties and dangers of the night. Today many Americans leave lights on in their homes when they are away, often with varying timer schemes, in order to discourage burglars. In big cities we shun the dark alleys and try to move only in groups and in "well lighted" areas during the darkness hours.

Children at an early age often develop a fear of darkness. Our adult fear of darkness is programmed into our young. When children are born, they do not fear darkness. Darkness is the norm in the environment from which they have emerged. As older children frighten young children in the dark and as stories about ghosts and monsters are told, a fear of the dark is developed. Especially strong programming forces develop from any cues that are received from adults. If a parent says or does anything that can be interpreted as a fear of the dark, it makes impressions on the child.

Throughout history darkness has been associated with evil, despair, and death. On the other hand, light and white have been associated with innocence, purity, joy, victory, and the supremacy of truth. This is a key reason why it is customary in our society to wear black or dark clothing to funerals and for brides to wear white.

Because of man's fear of darkness and its association with danger, many artificial sources of light have been developed. Primitive man kept fires burning at night as protection from those animals which attack in the dark. The forerunners of lighthouses were bonfires along the coast lines. Modern man spends millions of dollars on outdoor lighting. By creating artificial lights, man seeks to reduce the dangers and bondage of darkness.

During the 1970s many local governmental agencies heard complaints from their constituents as streetlights were changed to the more energy-efficient sodium-vapor types. Typical complaints included: crime will increase because the new lights do not illuminate as wide an area as the old lights; the lights are too dim for traffic safety; the lights are damaging to vegetation and have an adverse effect on humans psychologically.

As it turned out most of the complaints were simply not true. The sodium-vapor lights are just as bright and illuminate just as wide an area; in many cases brightness was increased, yet the complaints were heard. Neither has there been any supporting data regarding the harmful effects to life and happiness claims.

How do we explain the uproar over something which would be expected to receive a ground swell of support? After all, the purpose in switching to sodium-vapor streetlights was generally to save energy, which in turn translates into saved taxpayer dollars.

From a purely functional point of view, the actual composition of the lighting used in streetlights is not of importance. Because of high brightness levels with a corresponding relatively low level of energy input, sodium-vapor lights seem ideally suited for streets. Sodium lamps, however, emit most of their light in just two wavelengths, both of which are in the yellow region of the color spectrum. The lit area changes color rather dramatically in this yellow light. The artificial light produced from sodium has *distorted color* compared to our standard—sunlight. In the case of streetlights, this was particularly noticeable as the change was typically being made from mercury-vapor lamps, which have a bluish emphasis, to sodium-vapor with a yellowish emphasis.

Most photographers are familiar with the color distortion of artificial light. During the film era one brand of good color film had a bluish emphasis, while a different but equally as good color film emphasized the yellow spectrum. Many photographers chose their film based upon the subject they would be photographing and which colors they wanted to emphasize. Then and now some photographers use special filters to enhance certain colors to a greater extent. As a simple example, those wonderful scenics which contain fluffy white clouds against a truly deep blue sky are often obtained with a polarizing filter.

Photographers learned to monitor and control not only the color response characteristics of the film they were using, but more importantly the color temperature of the light striking their subject. This is extremely important since the color of anything we see depends not only upon the nature of the substance itself, but also upon the color of the light which is striking it. As we know, color is determined by which wavelengths of light reach our eyes.

When I was young aluminum-colored artificial Christmas trees were quite popular. A color wheel was often used to enhance the tree's beauty. The color wheel was nothing more than a light with a revolving wheel in front of it aimed at the tree. This revolving wheel contained a series of colored filters. As the wheel rotated, the various filters caused red light, green light, blue light, or amber light to strike the tree. The result was that the tree first appeared to be red, then green, then blue, and finally yellow. Since these filters were in a circular pattern on a revolving wheel, a sequence of constant color change occurred. The color we perceive an object to be is partly determined by the color of the light striking that object.

Artificial light has distorted color. Photographers of the past knew not to use outside color film when photographing inside with artificial lighting and expect to obtain accurate color reproductions. The incandescent lighting of our homes produces a yellow-orange emphasis. The mercury-vapor lights produce a bluish emphasis, and sodium-vapor lights are yellowish. Those of us who remember flash bulbs for cameras recall that they were available in the less expensive clear variety for black and white film, or with a blue coating which would "color correct" light for indoor use with outside film. Modern electronic flash units for cameras have been color corrected. Indoor color films were those in which the film itself responded well to the specific type of artificial lighting. Artificial light colors the world that it lights. It can change the appearance of an object significantly. Artificial light provides *distorted color.*

There is another significant difference between artificial light and sunlight. That difference is intensity. Man has never been able to produce a light which approaches the brightness, the intensity of our sun.

Application

There are many religions in the world today. Many stand for good, and at first glance may appear to be equivalent to the Son. Some of these "artificial lights" color the truth ever so slightly, and it is difficult to detect that they differ from the truth of God's Word. Some produce doctrines which are so different from God's Word that they are easier to discern.

The standard by which we measure artificial light is the sun. In spiritual light the standard by which we should compare artificial light is the Son. In both the physical and the spiritual, we know that the intensity of artificial light cannot even be compared with the true light. God is the all-powerful God. God is the true light.

The Book of First John has been a large part of the basis for this material. John wrote, "the darkness is passing away, and *the true light* is already shining" (1 John 2:8). Walking in the light is only possible now that the true light is seen. The contrast has changed in this portion of 1 John. It is no longer the difference between light and darkness, but rather now we see "the true light." The contrast now is between the true light and false or artificial lights.

The Old Testament psalmist knew of the protection that is available from the true God, the God who is light. "The Lord *is* my light and my salvation; whom shall I fear? The Lord *is* the strength of my life; of whom shall I be afraid?" (Psalm 27:1). "You shall not be afraid of the terror by night, nor of the arrow that flies by day, nor of the pestilence that walks in darkness, nor of the destruction that lays waste at noonday" (Psalm 91:5-6).

There is safety in the Cross of Calvary. Even though the Cross is a place of death, agony, horror, and suffering, it is a place of refuge and safety. You are now a recipient of that supreme sacrifice. You can now become a child of light. The Cross provides protection for the sinner from the wrath of a holy and righteous God.

Sunlight / Sonlight

Artificial lights typically are of a different intensity and they emphasize color differently than sunlight.

Man-made religions are of different intensities than Sonlight and their emphasis is often different than Sonlight.

THINK AND GROW

1. Does your belief system align with the Word of God and Sonlight?

2. Are you protected from the wrath of a holy God by the true light of Christ?

11

Mirages:

Distorted Image

Artificial light, as we have seen, does not provide an accurate image because of incomplete or distorted color. We come now to mirages, which provide an inaccurate image because of distorted light. By distorted light we mean the individual rays of light which we receive have been so twisted as to no longer represent the original image correctly. The individual light rays which make up the whole are no longer in the same relationship one to another. With a mirage it is very easy to fall into a delusion or a snare.

Perhaps the classic of all such delusions is the tired desert traveler who believes he sees a lake in the distance (sometimes a mirage of a complete oasis is seen). This is not imaginary, nor is it "his mind playing tricks on him." The traveler really does perceive water. One of the real ironies of mirages is that we are most inclined to see phantom water in the most heat-drenched, arid places. When the exhausted traveler is most in need of cool refreshment, he is most prone to experience the mirage of a body of water.

We have all experienced a mirage at one time or another. We have all ridden in an automobile on a sunny day and experienced the mirage of puddles of water on the highway. As we continued down the highway, the puddles disappeared before our very eyes. These puddles of water were never there. But you did perceive them with your vision. The water was a mirage; it was an optical illusion.

How does a mirage occur? Dark surfaces absorb light. As light is absorbed, heat is produced and causes "heat waves" to rise off the hot object. When a highway, particularly a black asphalt highway, is exposed to hot direct sunlight, the road surface is elevated in temperature. A layer of air immediately above the road surface becomes quite warm, but higher off the ground the air remains relatively cool. These layers of air (different transparent mediums) cause light to be refracted or bent. Remember that light is bent slightly as it crosses the boundary of two differing transparent mediums. Since the cooler air in our example is denser than the heated air just above the road surface, we have different transparent mediums and a bending of light.

The rays of light that are traveling nearly horizontal, almost parallel to the ground but slightly downward, are bent slightly so that they now are traveling slightly upward towards the observer. These rays appear to the observer as if they were coming from the ground.

But we still need to explain the appearance of water. We have all noticed distant pools of real water. Close observation of such a pool of water reveals that the pool is reflecting rays of light from the sky to the distant observer. Light rays from the sky are bounced off, or reflected from, the pool and upwards towards the observer's eye. What the eye perceives is a bright spot of light that appears to be on the ground. Experience has taught us that such bright areas are bodies of water. What is happening is light from the sky is being reflected off the water's surface to our eyes.

When we see a mirage puddle on the highway ahead, we are seeing a very similar bright area, but this time caused by refraction in the air instead of reflection off the water. It looks identical to sunlight being reflected off water, and so we have every reason to believe it is caused by water.

Earlier we referenced the classic mirage of the desert traveler. The desert mirage is caused in the same way as the highway mirage. Weary travelers are often fooled by the illusion, even if they understand the nature and cause of what they were seeing. The mirage is so complete and convincing that it fools even those who know better. Many such people have persisted in the disillusionment until it helped speed their death. It is interesting to note that many experienced desert travelers report that animals are never deceived by a mirage.

There are other forms of mirages which are just as real to those who observe them as the water mirage. Some of these are much more complicated to explain simply. In one type of a mirage trees and houses appear in the sky, often high above the horizon. In a very real way, this type of sky mirage is just the reverse of a water mirage. With the sky mirage there is often an enlarging or magnified effect. It can be very startling and eerie to see enlarged images of trees or buildings floating in the sky.

The "twinkling" of stars is caused in a similar way to a mirage. As light which is of constant brightness travels to us, it passes through many currents of air in our earth's atmosphere. Parts of the air are quite cool and other parts substantially warmer. These air currents are in motion. The light from the stars is bent or refracted as it passes between these currents of air. The more these different temperature zones of air are moving, the more the light from the star tends to shift about, producing the "twinkling."

Mirages produce a distorted image. What we see is not an accurate image of what is there. A distorted image can be produced in other ways besides a mirage.

A highly reflective material, whether it is opaque, translucent, or transparent, may provide a distorted image. To obtain an accurate image by reflection the surface must be flat. In the case of a clear transparent material, the surface must be flat and of uniform thickness in order to provide an accurate image. Otherwise the result will be a distorted image.

One common example of a distorted reflected image is the funhouse or arcade mirror. Typically, this type of mirror is bent into a gently curving shape along the vertical edges. Depending upon the observer's height and where he stands in relation to the mirror, various distorted images are seen.

Clear transparent materials which are not flat nor of uniform thickness also produce a changed (or distorted) image. If this were not so, we would not have the optical systems of our era. Camera lenses and other optical systems are evidence of man's acquired knowledge to put various such individual lenses together into a system for useful application.

Application

Mirages produce distorted images. The way that a distorted image is produced is by distorting light or changing the relationships between component parts of the light. There are many groups who want to distort or change the relationship of the true light. Jesus Christ was the True Light of this world. He was the "Living Word." John begins his gospel with reference to Jesus Christ as the Living Word, "In the beginning was the Word, and the Word was with God, and the Word was God. He was in the beginning with God. All things were made through Him, and without Him nothing was made that was made. In Him was life, and the life was the light of men. And the light shines in the darkness, and the darkness did not comprehend it" (John 1:1-5).

Today we have the testimony about the living Word and we also have the written Word of God. There are groups who would change the relationship of component parts of God's Word, thereby distorting the truth.

Some groups would mix a doctrine of works into salvation. The Bible does teach works, but not in connection with salvation. The apostle

Paul wrote, "For by grace you have been saved through faith, and that not of yourselves; it is the gift of God, not of works, lest anyone should boast" (Ephesians 2:8-9). And in Timothy we find, "Who has saved us and called us with a holy calling, not according to our works, but according to His own purpose and grace which was given to us in Christ Jesus before time began" (2 Timothy 1:9). Our doing good, our own righteousness, has no part in salvation. However, it is also clear from Scripture that good works are a *result* of salvation. Matthew wrote, "Let your light so shine before men, that they may see your good works and glorify your Father in heaven" (Matthew 5:16).

There are those who would teach that "God is love" and therefore all of mankind will escape punishment. The Bible does indeed teach that "God is love," but it also clearly teaches that God is a God of wrath who hates sin, and that there is coming a day of accountability and reckoning. The Ephesian church was warned about God's hatred of sin, "because of such things God's wrath comes on those who are disobedient" (Ephesians 5:6 niv). The children of light and obedience at Colosse were warned in a similar manner, "Because of these things [sins just listed in the context] the wrath of God is coming upon the sons of disobedience" (Colossians 3:6). As a child of light, you will escape the coming wrath of God. Instead of a fearful wrath in your future, you look forward to the return of Jesus Christ. Your responsibility is "to serve the living and true God, and to wait for His Son from heaven, whom He raised from the dead, even Jesus who delivers us from the wrath to come" (1 Thessalonians 1:9-10).

Groups which teach the truth in a distorted manner are analogous to a mirage. As in the case of physical light, these teachings can appear very real. But just as in physical mirages, they have no reality. Just as in the case of physical light mirages, where many are deluded, even many who know better, so too regarding spiritual mirages. And as in the case of the physical, the final result of being deceived may well be death.

How do you avoid being deceived by a spiritual mirage?

First, you need to understand that they exist. Second, you must not underestimate the convincing nature of a mirage. (Many individuals who were caught up in the Jonestown massacre were convinced they were following the truth.) Third, you need to personally exercise the options that are available to you. You need to spend time in Bible study, prayer, and meditation.

The most important step of all is simple faith in Jesus Christ as Savior. Once you have become a child of light, there are guards which need to be personally used. Regular prayer and Bible study are essential. The Holy Spirit of God, the third member of the Trinity, is available to the child of light to teach you and direct your path. "But the Helper, the Holy Spirit, whom the Father will send in My name, He will teach you all things, and bring to your remembrance all things that I said to you" (John 14:26).

Sunlight / Sonlight

Distorted images of sunlight appear real and deceive the observer. The result can be physical death.

Distorted images of Sonlight appear real and deceive many. The result can be spiritual death.

THINK AND GROW

1. Does the church with which you are associated teach a distorted image of Sonlight?

2. Are you protected from spiritual mirages?

12

Shadows:

Distorted Intensity

We have seen that substitute or artificial lights that provide *distorted color* and mirages produce a *distorted image*. In this chapter we consider shadows, which provide a reduced brightness or *distorted intensity*.

Shadows can be useful. When light is intense and shadows are present, our vision is increased and we have an accurate perception of reality. This contrast of brighter light and reduced light is very helpful in understanding the reality of our environment—for example, it is easy to see ridges and depressions. Championship skiers refer to "flat light," which can occur on very overcast days. This is not a "white-out" condition of strong snow or fog, but rather the lack of shadows, causing the surroundings to appear uniform. Even the sky can blend with the snow under the skier's feet in these conditions and rises and depressions are extremely difficult to see.

The normal contrast provided by varying intensity of light increases our depth perception. While flying with a bush pilot in Alaska, our family learned that the pilots carry evergreen boughs with them in their planes in case of very "flat light" conditions. In such times, it is very difficult to judge their distance above the ground. Dropping the branches onto the snow below enables them to determine the distance to the ground.

Application

The Word of God has much to say about shadows. Shadows are mentioned with respect to prophecy or foreshadowing of that which is to come. For instance, in Colossians the Jewish law was said to be "a shadow of things to come" (Colossians 2:17). A shadow is indistinct because of the reduced light. A shadow does not provide detail, but only the silhouette of that which is being shadowed. The law was a shadow of things to come. Jesus said, "Do not think that I came to destroy the Law or the Prophets. I did not come to destroy but to fulfill" (Matthew 5:17). The life of Jesus Christ exhibited the beauty of the law, while the death of Jesus Christ met the demands of the law. The Old Testament law was a foreshadowing of Christ. The Jewish law was "a shadow of things to come."

Shadows provide proof that there is a light source. Both sunlight and Sonlight create shadows.

Shadows are not the genuine item. The writer of Hebrews explains the role of the law: "The law is only a shadow of the good things that are coming—not the realities themselves" (Hebrews 10:1 niv). We are told that the law can never make anyone perfect or sinless. Indeed, the law shows that we are imperfect and sinful.

The writer of Hebrews portrays the Aaronic priests of the Old Testament as shadows of Christ, who is the reality. Jesus Christ is the true high priest. Regarding earthly priests we are told that "They serve at a sanctuary that is a copy and shadow of what is in heaven" (Hebrews 8:5). It is Jesus Christ who is the true high priest. Jesus Christ is the light of the world. As a child of light you are to reflect the light of Christ to the darkness around you.

An object does not reflect light unless the object is in the light. John wrote, "But if we walk in the light as He is in the light, we have fellowship with one another, and the blood of Jesus Christ His Son cleanses us from all sin" (1 John 1:7). To be a light in this world it is important that you yourself are walking in the light. The apostle John in writing to children of light makes it clear that it is possible to walk in darkness. You can walk in shadows. "The darkness is passing away, and the true light is already shining. He who says he is in the light, and hates his brother, is in darkness until now. He who loves his brother abides in the light, and there is no cause for stumbling in him. But he who hates his brother is in darkness and walks in darkness, and does not know where he is going, because the darkness has blinded his eyes" (1 John 2:8-11). This passage makes it clear that it is possible to step out of the light and into a shadow.

What causes a child of light to be in the shadow? John tells us "if we walk in the light, as He is in the light, we have fellowship with one another," and John has also made it clear that "our fellowship is with the Father and with His Son, Jesus Christ" (1 John 1:3 niv). When you are in fellowship with God, His presence is a very real part of your daily walk. God's presence brings with it the consciousness of your sinful nature. His presence also brings to your conscience any sin in your life. Sin is what separates man from God. Unconfessed sin causes the child of light to step into the shadow. Sin in the spiritual realm is analogous to darkness in the physical world. Once you are a child of light, sin which is unconfessed is the thing which interrupts your spiritual light. The only thing that can interrupt physical light is the shadow caused by something opaque separating an object from the light source. It is most encouraging to note, however, that light penetrates darkness. Darkness cannot overcome light. The victory belongs to the child of God if you are willing to put yourself back in the light.

How can a child of God who has slipped into the shadow of sin be put back into the unobstructed light? "If we confess our sins, He is faithful and just and will forgive us our sins and purify us from all unrighteousness" (1 John 1:9).

One Saturday I decided that it was time to clean all the windows in our home. I spent several hours, cleaning each glass surface very carefully, followed by a second careful cleaning. The outdoors had never seemed so much a part of our home as it did that late afternoon. The windows were spotless.

The next morning upon entering the living room I was in for a real shock. The east-facing window was dirty! The morning sun revealed that it was indeed dirty. There was one spot that I had somehow missed, and there were also some dirty streaks on other parts of the window. How could this be?

Checking windows for cleanliness is one thing when the windows are in the shade, it is quite another when they are in the full sunlight! "But all things that are exposed are made manifest by the light, for whatever makes manifest is light" (Ephesians 5:13).

For the child of God who has slipped into the shade it is important to be restored, through the confession of known sin, into the full Sonlight. A stark reality, however, is that once we are back in the full Sonlight, we are going to see additional areas of our lives which need the application of 1 John 1:9. Failure to do so will cause the shadow of broken fellowship to again engulf us. Shadows are caused by allowing something to come between us and the light source. Unconfessed sin will come between a "child of light" and the God who is light.

When a child of light is separated from direct contact with the source of light, it is an instance of broken fellowship, not broken relationship. We have been born into God's family. We cannot be unborn spiritually just as we cannot be unborn physically. Jesus Christ, likening the children of light to sheep, said, "And I give them eternal life, and they shall never perish; neither shall anyone snatch them out of My hand. My Father, who has given them to Me, is greater than all; and no one is able to snatch them out of My Father's hand" (John 10:28-29). Relationship with God is not a question once we have been born into the family. Fellowship with the Father and the Son can be broken by unconfessed sin in the life. Broken fellowship is like being in the shadow.

"Robert Louis Stevenson tells a vivid story of a storm at sea. The passengers below were greatly alarmed, as the waves dashed over the vessel. At last one of them, against orders, crept to the deck, and came to the pilot, who was lashed to the wheel which he was turning without flinching. The pilot caught sight of the terror-stricken man and gave him a reassuring smile. Below went the passenger, and comforted the others by saying, 'I have seen the face of the pilot, and he smiled. All is well.'

"That is how we feel when through the gateway of prayer we find our way into the Father's presence. We see His face, and we know that all is well, since His hand is on the helm of events, and 'even the winds and the waves obey Him.' When we live in fellowship with Him, we come with confidence into His presence, asking in the full confidence of receiving and meeting with the justification of our faith."[6]

There is a great truth in that story. The only way to keep sin from ruling our lives is to confess sin immediately and to see the face of our pilot. We have the Old Testament example of David: "I foresaw the Lord always before my face, for He is at my right hand, that I may not be shaken" (Acts 2:25). David knew the value of keeping God in front of his face.

The New Testament writer to the Hebrews wrote, "Let us run with endurance the race that is set before us, looking unto Jesus, the author and finisher of our faith" (Hebrews 12:1-2). Later in that same chapter we are told, "Follow peace with all men, and holiness ... looking diligently lest any man fail..." (Hebrews 12:14-15 kjv). If we are to maintain fellowship with our Father, we must be looking steadfastly towards His Son.

The right direction of vision is important. First, notice that you are never in the shadow when you are facing the light. Helen Keller put it this way, "Keep your face to the sunshine and you cannot see a shadow." In other words, the shadows always fall behind the person who is walking towards the light. Second, the direction we are facing has a lot to do with progress towards our destination. A third reason is the strong rebuke that our Master gave Peter in the last chapter of John's gospel.

Recall that the Lord had been having a very personal and serious discussion with Simon Peter. Peter gave all the right answers but did not stop to contemplate the meaning of the words. Then Peter turned to our Lord and inquired what His plans were for the apostle John. Peter asked, "But Lord, what about this man?" (John 21:21). Jesus very succinctly told Peter, in effect, it is none of your business, Peter, what My plans are for John. You, Peter, be sure that you are faithful. Peter, you follow Me!

That rebuke to Peter by our Lord should make it very clear that we are not to compare ourselves to each other. The standard is Christ. How do we measure up against Christ? How much of Christ are we reflecting to those around us in darkness?

All that we have, we have received from Christ. Your talents, gifts, and abilities have been given to you from God Himself. Where is there any room for boasting? Where is there any reason to compare yourself against another? There is no reason for either an inferiority or a superiority complex. All that you are, you have been given by your Creator. "Every good and perfect gift is from above, coming down from the Father of the heavenly lights, who does not change like shifting shadows" (James 1:17 niv). God is the source of all that we have. God is the great unchanging One. God does not have a shifting shadow. If you are a child of light and are now in a shadow, it is not that God, the light source, has moved, but rather a problem of unconfessed sin in your life. It is up to you by confession of sin to take the step that restores you into the full brilliance of Sonlight. Jesus said, "I have come as a light into the world, that whoever believes in Me should not abide in darkness" (John 12:46).

Sunlight / Sonlight

The shadows of sunlight can be very useful, or they can be dangerous—in either case they are not the real thing.

The shadows of Sonlight can be very useful or they can be dangerous—in either case they are not the real thing.

THINK AND GROW

1. Are you currently walking in the shadow of unconfessed sin?

2. Are you basking in the full brightness of Sonlight?

3. Are you currently gazing into the face of your Pilot? Is everything well?

13

Luminescence: Living Light

It was a warm August night in the state of Georgia and I was lying in a sleeping bag near some trees, looking up into the clear sky. My eyeglasses had been put away safely for the night. As I gazed into the night sky, countless stars were shining brightly.

A meteor streaked across the sky, but surprisingly it seemed to take a curved path! On many previous occasions, particularly in August, I had experienced the wonder of meteor showers in the sky. Never in my experience had a meteor taken such a curved path. Suddenly another curving meteor caught my attention, and then another, and another.

I reached for my eyeglasses and because of my commotion, Hans, my companion, was awakened after having just dropped off to sleep. My glasses were on now and I could see that my eyes were not playing tricks on me. Hans laughed heartily as I explained what was happening. As soon as Hans mentioned the word *fireflies,* I realized that these were not distant meteors but little insects only a few feet up in the air.

It is difficult for me to express my inner excitement the first time I experienced *living light.* My life had previously been sheltered from *bioluminescence.* I have since learned that although the firefly's light is not bright, these little insects convert almost one hundred percent of the energy they use into light (only a very small portion of the energy is changed into heat). It would take almost 140,000 fireflies to equal the light produced by an ordinary 60-watt light bulb. Although the light given by the firefly is small, it thrills the first-time observer with amazement at the insect's beauty and provides the observer with a sense of wonder and awe.

We need to briefly define some interrelated terms. *Luminescence* is the ability to emit light that is not directly related to heat (fire and artificial lights are *not* luminescent). A characteristic of all luminescence is that very little or no heat is produced. There are several categories of luminescence.

Fluorescence is luminescence that occurs *while* an external stimulus is active. Fluorescent materials typically fluoresce or produce certain specific wavelengths of light. A fluorescent light stops glowing when the electricity is turned off. Fluorescent tubes get their energy from electrons in electricity.

Phosphorescence on the other hand is the type of luminescence that occurs *after* an external stimulus such as sunlight has been active. Phosphorescent light keeps glowing after the energy is turned off. Phosphorescent objects get their energy directly from light; they store energy—almost like a miniature battery. The glow on the radium dials of old-fashioned watches comes from phosphorescence. Traditional television sets used phosphorescence to provide the picture. Today in our digital world we speak freely of pixels which are individual units which glow.

Chemiluminescence describes the glow that is caused from chemical sources of energy. "Light sticks" that some trick-or-treaters use at Halloween is an example.

Mechanical luminescence is the glow caused by mechanical energy. For example, the simple crushing of a sugar cube in a dark room will excite electrons so that they emit photons, causing the bits of sugar to glow.

Bioluminescence is *living light* and a common example is fireflies. Fireflies are by no means the only example of bioluminescence. The smallest producers of light in the world as far as we know are bacteria. Many various types of bacteria emit light, in the air, on land, and in the sea.

In the sea we find many cases of luminescence. Many *living lights* are very small, as in the cases of bacteria and fungi. In the sea tiny microscopic marine animals called protozoa exhibit the property of luminescence. But in sea life, as elsewhere, luminescence is not reserved for the very small. For example, some varieties of shellfish, shrimp, crab, squid, and even some sharks exhibit a luminescence. Scientists at Scripps Institute of Oceanography estimate that about eighty percent of all marine life exhibits this *glow-in-the-water* ability.

In New Zealand my wife and I were privileged to take a boat tour through the Waitomo Glowworm Caves which were utterly fascinating. These limestone caves are famous for the glowworms which emit light to attract food.

There are also many types of insects, such as the firefly and the glowworm (which is in reality a beetle), that produce light. The common earthworm emits a small amount of luminescence, but it is difficult to detect. The centipede is luminescent, and there are luminescent fleas. Scorpions, also luminescent, are hunted by scientists at night with black (ultraviolet) light. The scorpions give off a greenish glow when the black light strikes them.

Bioluminescence appears to be concentrated entirely within the visible portion of the electromagnetic spectrum. At the violet end of the visible light spectrum is the bioluminescence exhibited in the sea. The sea's bioluminescence extends on into the blue and green regions. Bacterial light is in the blue range, towards the greenish end. The luminescent light of fungi peaks in the green region. The firefly's light is in the orange portion of the spectrum towards the yellow end. The railroad worm gives a red-orange light from the orange region of the color spectrum. "Note that no bioluminescence ranges down to the lowermost visible red, where it fades into infra-red, and none ranges as high as the uppermost visible violet, where it fades into ultra-violet. Bioluminescence, as emphasized again here, is concentrated in the frequencies which stimulate sight reactions in the eyes of most living creatures, human or animal."[7]

Besides bioluminescence, there are other types of luminescence in nature. There are many luminescent plants, such as nasturtium, marigold, poppy, and the sunflower. Several light-emitting woods are known. There are many luminescent bacteria as well as many varieties of luminescent fungi. Sometimes an electric luminescence is exhibited. Under certain conditions luminescent raindrops, snowflakes, and even hailstones have been reported. Usually this phenomenon is seen during or following thunderstorms.

In the mineral world we find more examples of luminescence. Common limestone has a phosphorescent ability, as do many more exotic mineral bodies, including certain diamonds. Who has not at one time or another thrilled to the phosphorescence of rock samples being exposed to *black light* in a dark room? Many of these reactions are a chemical luminescence.

Objects that glow do so because they emit photons of light—little bundles of energy. Blue photons have the most energy, red the least. There are other photons besides light photons, such as radio photons and X-ray photons. The only real difference between light photons and other photons is that light photons are the ones we can see. However, the energy may be from a variety of sources.

Only a portion of creation can emit light through the process called luminescence. This is true within all three classifications of material objects—animal, vegetable, and mineral. The amount of light they produce is infinitesimally small when compared to their source of light. Nevertheless, light is produced by a portion of creation.

Our eyes contain a special molecule called rhodopsin, which acts as a radio antenna tuned to pick up light photons. The tail of a rhodopsin molecule is normally bent, but when it receives the photon, the photon's energy causes the tail to straighten out and break off. The broken-off tail is called "opsin," a small molecule which in effect tells our nerves, "I've seen a photon."

Sight is a continuous cycle of building rhodopsin, opsin being torn off, and opsin being put back on again. But that reassembly takes a moment. That is why you are temporarily blind when you walk into a dark room from the bright sunlight. Rhodopsin breaks down so rapidly in the sunlight that it takes a few moments in a dark room for enough rhodopsin to be put back together so you can see.

Application

In previous chapters we have seen that we owe our very existence to the light that we receive from the sun. In one way it seems strange that only a *portion* of creation responds by emitting light itself! It is another analogy regarding the spiritual. Jesus Christ, the light of the world, died for all of mankind. He died that all might be saved. Jesus Christ is the true light in a dark world. Yet only a small percentage have accepted the provision of the Cross. Only a portion of mankind has become children of light. Only a fraction of humanity is spiritually luminescent.

Bioluminescence is much more prevalent in tropical zones. Where light is strongest, bioluminescence is more prevalent. As a child of light you are to *live in the light* if you are to emit light to your surroundings.

There is an analogy between man's response to spiritual light and the response of the plant world to physical light. Botanists know that plants can be divided into three classes. These classes are related to various plants' reactions to the length of day. The variable is what percentage of the time the plant is in daylight.

The first group of plants will flower only if there is in excess of a certain amount of sunlight. A typical example would be the many summer-flowering annuals and biennials. These plants do not bloom during other times in the year. For their true beauty to be shown, these plants need lots of sunlight.

The second group of plants will only flower if the amount of daylight is less than a certain amount. Examples of this group are the autumn-flowering annuals. During summer months this category of plants grows but does not produce flowers. They begin to produce flowers when the sunlight hours are shortened. The true beauty of this group of plants is not seen until darker days come.

There is another group of plants. These plants are predictable regardless of the amount of sunlight. This group includes many vegetables, including cucumbers and potatoes. Many of the plants in this group will produce flowers even if grown in total darkness.

These three groups of plants, it would seem, may have counterparts *within the children of light.* First, there are those individuals who blossom into what they should be only when they are basking heavily in heavenly Sonlight. Such an individual quits blooming if separated from regular Christian fellowship, or if regular daily prayer and Bible study are missed. The solar collectors that heat the water in some homes are like these individuals. When there is sufficient sunlight, they work great. The moment the incoming light is blocked by heavy shadows or hours of darkness, the collectors become useless. Many of our high-tech devices of today which utilize pixels also fall into this category.

As in the second group of plants, there are those children of light who appear to be growing consistently, but do not seem to live up to their potential. An observer senses that they could be so much more. Then something causes them to blossom just like our second group of plants. There have been many accounts given of individuals who when in prison or enduring other hardship have blossomed beautifully. Sometimes the removal of Christian fellowship and the lack of the written Word of God has caused individuals to blossom forth.

Thankfully, there is also that third group, those who blossom and live up to their potential no matter what the external circumstances are. The sun keeps shining twenty-four hours a day, seven days a week, every week. The sun doesn't change its brightness level based upon external factors, such as relative position to the earth or other planets. The sun is the physical light of the world. Jesus Christ, the Son, is the spiritual light of the world. He is our example. Perhaps one of the greatest contrasts between Christ's life and our lives was His absolute consistency. Jesus Christ is seeking those who will follow Him.

Sunlight / Sonlight

In the physical world there are many examples of living lights resulting from sunlight.

In the spiritual world there are many examples of living lights resulting from Sonlight.

THINK AND GROW

1. Are you a living light? Are you sure—beyond any doubt?

2. Are you consistently blooming regardless of outward circumstances?

3. Are you living up to your potential? Are you consistently blossoming? Do you emit the fragrance of Sonlight?

14

Binary:

One or the Other

In a prior eBook *GOD'S NATURE: Sonlight—Sunlight* we discussed the concept of duality. We saw that light can be explained adequately only by attributing two natures to it. Light apparently is made up of particles or packets of energy *and* waves at the same time. No one fully understands how this can be, yet scientists accept it as true. Both explanations are necessary to satisfy the known behavior of light. We observed a parallel between the duality of physical light and the duality of spiritual light. Jesus Christ was fully and completely man, while simultaneously fully and completely God. No one understands how this can be, yet theologians accept it as true. Both explanations are necessary to satisfy the known nature of God in the form of Jesus Christ. The Word of God clearly teaches this duality. *Duality* is the state or condition of being *both at once*. Both sunlight and Sonlight have dual natures.

Duality and Binary

Furthermore, physical objects react to sunlight in a *binary* manner. Humans react to Sonlight in a binary manner. *Duality is both at once and binary is one or the other.*

We live in a *binary* world. The word binary also denotes two. Something that is binary is made up of or characterized by having two parts, or two conditions. Modern computers have a profound effect on our lives. Computers run on the binary system of mathematics. Instead of the ten numbers with which we are used to working, the binary system uses only two numbers, zero and one. Tiny little "bits" of information are being differentiated inside today's computers as either *zero* or *one*. A bit of information is either *on* or *off*. In the terminology of today's high technology society, *binary* denotes the state or condition of being on or off, zero or one, *one* or *the other*.

The speed and performance of modern computers are increasing at an astonishing rate—as a result computers now affect our lives in many ways every day. Computerized billing systems remind us regularly of our obligations. Computerized traffic control systems manage our transportation systems. Modern automobiles have multiple computers managing such aspects as engine performance and modern safety systems. Computers are being used in increasingly useful ways including in the design and manufacture of products. Computerized video games have fascinated our society. Computers aid law enforcement officers, while posing new challenges regarding computer data crimes. Computers have invaded our lives and the rate of change is accelerating.

One of the important specifications of any computer is its "memory size." This is a measurement of how many bits of information the computer can store at one time. The great decrease in computer memory cost and the subsequent increase in computer memory capacities are prime reasons for the rapid acceleration in computer applications. There has also been a significant decrease in physical size in computers and their memories.

Humans have their own built-in computers. "The information content of the human brain expressed in bits is probably comparable to the total number of connections among the neurons—about a hundred trillion, 10^{14}, bits. If written out in English, say, that information would fill some twenty million volumes, as many as in the world's largest libraries. The equivalent of twenty million books is inside the heads of every one of us. The brain is a very big place in a very small space."[8] With all our great technological advances, there is something very humbling about stepping back and realizing the extreme complexity of all of creation. David wrote: "I will praise You because I am fearfully *and* wonderfully made; marvelous are Your works, and *that* my soul knows very well" (Psalm 139:14).

We have been considering reactions to light. There are many binary reactions to light, reactions that are this *or* that.

Attracted or Repelled

There is a phenomenon called *photophoresis* that was discovered by the Viennese physicist Professor Felix Ehrenhaft. This phenomenon is another example of behavior that is different than that to which we are accustomed. Normally when something is hit by some force, its tendency is to move away from the force. We expect something that has been hit to move in the same direction as the force was heading when it struck the object. As we have previously noted, light from our sun strikes the surface of the earth with a measurable force.

"Although this pressure exerted by light is simple enough to understand, there is a phenomenon connected with it that remains an unsolved mystery. This is the movement of small particles in opposite directions when a beam of light falls on them. Some particles move away from the source of light, as might be expected if pressure is exerted on them; others, however, move towards the source of the light, as though they were being attracted to it."[9] In other words, some particles are attracted to the source of the light, while other particles are repelled away from the source of the light.

Electrons move varying distances when light strikes an object. Blue photons have the most energy because their electrons move the greatest distance. The electrons of red photons move the shortest distance and hence have the least energy.

A similar reaction is seen in living creatures. There are many nocturnal plants and animals—those which are of the night. Coyotes, wolves, koalas, and raccoons are examples. Some creatures of the night actively pursue artificial light when it is available. "Many marine animals are attracted to our underwater lights. Tiny fishes and worms batter themselves to death against the glass lenses, striving as relentlessly as moths against a naked lightbulb. Why? We don't know. During the day these same creatures hide away, shunning the light. Yet at evening they come forth in their millions, their passion for light so great that they give their lives for a few seconds of cold white illumination."[10]

The analogy is clear. In our physical world some living things are attracted to the true Light and others are nocturnal. There exist both moths which are attracted to light and cockroaches which run from the light. So too in the spiritual world.

Mocking or Listening

In this binary situation of attraction or repulsion, it is the question of acceptance or rejection. "And when they heard of the resurrection of the dead, some mocked, while others said, 'We will hear you again on this matter.' So Paul departed from among them. However, some men joined him and believed, among them Dionysius the Areopagite, a woman named Damaris, and others with them" (Acts 17:32-34). Some were mocking while others were believing.

Protection or Conviction

Light is protective, as we have repeatedly seen. Light manifests or reveals what is already there. This is true for both physical light and spiritual light. "This is the verdict: Light has come into the world, but men loved darkness instead of light, because their deeds were evil. Everyone who does evil hates the light, and will not come into the light, for fear that his deeds will be exposed. But whoever lives by the truth comes into the light, so that it may be seen plainly that what he has done has been done through God" (John 3:19-21 niv).

Softening or Hardening

The same sun that melts the snow hardens the soft mud into hard barren ground. When the Pharisees asked Jesus for a sign, He responded at one point with questions, each of which stated its own answer: "Do you not yet perceive nor understand? Is your heart still hardened? Having eyes, do you not see? And having ears, do you not hear? And do you not remember?" ... 'How is it you do not understand?'" (Mark 8:17b-18, 21b).

The sun can *harden* or *soften*. You can listen to the words of the Son and be hardened or softened. You can look, but through spiritual blindness not observe. You can listen but not hear.

~ *Quote* ~ "The same sun which melts was hardens clay. And the same Gospel which melts some persons to repentance hardens others in their sins." —C.H. Spurgeon

Cleansing or Rotting

Decay occurs at an increasing pace if we rebel. A child of light should be growing in purity and holiness. Jesus Christ commanded His followers, "You also be holy in all your conduct ... *Be holy, for I am holy*" (1 Peter 1:15-16). The greatest incentive to a righteous life is the second coming of Christ. The "blessed hope" of the child of light should lead to purification. "Everyone who has this hope in him purifies himself, just as He is pure" (1 John 3:3).

On the other hand, those who refuse to allow the cleansing Sonlight to penetrate and purge are in a state of decay and corruption. In warning of false doctrines that deny the truth of salvation in the blood of Jesus Christ, Peter wrote that those who teach this "blaspheme in matters they do not understand. They are like brute beasts, creatures of instinct, born only to be caught and destroyed, and like beasts they too will perish. They will be paid back with harm for the harm they have done" (2 Peter 2:12-13 niv). Peter goes on to warn about many false teachers in the name of Christian liberty. "While they promise them liberty, they themselves are slaves of corruption; for by whom a person is overcome, by him also he is brought into bondage" (2 Peter 2:19). The true children of light, however, "participate in the divine nature and escape the corruption in the world caused by evil desires" (2 Peter 1:4 niv).

Sweet Fragrance or Foul Stench

This may sound like a radical statement. But this contrast is straight from the Word of God. "Our lives are a *Christ-like fragrance* rising up to God. But this fragrance is perceived differently by those who are being saved and by those who are perishing. To those who are perishing, we are a *dreadful smell of death and doom*. But to those who are being saved, we are a *life-giving perfume*" (2 Corinthians 2:15-16a nlt, emphasis added).

Growth or Death

We know that the physical sun gives light, and in so doing provides life, but sunstroke can cause death. "As for man, his days are like grass" (Psalm 103:15) is literally true. Not only is his life short in relation to eternity but his sustenance is dependent on plant growth. The weary desert traveler without water soon finds only death. The same is true with spiritual life. Jesus said, "I have come that they may have life, and that they may have it more abundantly" (John 10:10). Jesus also clearly taught that those who fail to acknowledge Him will be condemned. "He who believes in the Son has everlasting life; and he who does not believe the Son shall not see life, but the wrath of God abides on him"

(John 3:36). Healthy growing plants turn toward the light. Rotting dead plants are consumed. The choice is between growth and death.

Religion or Relationship

In the realm of spiritual light we find the binary reaction of *belief* or *unbelief.* The issue is not really one of belief but whether an individual chooses to believe the *true* or *false.* It is a question of *religion* or *relationship* with Jesus Christ. It is the understanding that the Cross of Calvary paid the price of sin and it is the difference between *do* or *done.* The Christian faith understands we cannot do anything for merit, but rather it has been done by Christ. It is the choice of believing the great gurus and their ideology or believing the Son of God. There is only one way to gain eternal life. Jesus Christ, the Son of God, is different from all others—consider, for example, any social event. It is quite proper to quote from Ghandi, Mohammed, Confucius, or Buddha, but it is not politically correct to bring up Jesus Christ—except to use His name in vain. None of those other names is used routinely in cursing. How can we account for these facts? The only explanation is that "Light has come into the world, and men loved darkness rather than light, because their deeds were evil. For everyone practicing evil hates the light and does not come to the light, lest his deeds should be exposed" (John 3:19-20).

Heaven or Hell

The most important binary factor to consider is our final destiny, *heaven* or *hell.* In previous writings we saw how heaven will be filled with His light. Christ is the source of all light. Is it possible that hell will be eternal darkness? I don't know. The traditional view of hell consisting of unending fire may be more symbolic of eternal torture and lament rather than of literal flames—perhaps it is a metaphor of a burning anguished conscience—never to be extinguished—which regrets how life was lived. Perhaps hell is an endless review of what was done wrong—poetic justice for those too proud to trust in the Savior. One thing we do know for sure about heaven is that it is a place of light and possesses the ultimate source of light, Christ Himself. We also know that hell is in direct contrast to heaven.

The Book of Psalms holds an interesting description of the result of those who live for the present rather than for eternal values. "Hear this, all peoples; give ear, all inhabitants of the world, both low and high, rich and poor together. My mouth will speak wisdom; and the meditation of my heart will be understanding. I will incline my ear to a proverb; I will express my riddle on the harp ... Even those who trust in their wealth, and boast in the abundance of their riches ... even wise men die; the stupid and the senseless alike perish, and leave their wealth to others. Their inner thought is, that their houses are forever, and their dwelling places to all generations; they have called their lands after their own names. But man in his pomp will not endure; he is like the beasts that perish ... Do not be afraid when a man becomes rich, when the glory of his house is increased, for when he dies he will carry nothing away; his glory will not descend after him. Though while he lives he congratulates himself—and though men praise you when you do well for yourself—he shall go to the generation of his fathers; *they shall never see the light.* Man in his pomp, yet without understanding is like the beasts that perish" (Psalm 49:1-4, 6, 10-12, 16-20 nasb).

Application

We have looked at various reactions to light that are binary (there are many other binary pairs that could be reviewed). You can be either attracted or repelled by the true light of this world. You choose to mock or listen. Light can be either protective or convicting. Your heart can be softened; or by refusing to respond, you can be hardened by the truth. Divine light should cause cleansing; but if you refuse to hearken, it allows further rotting. The choice is to emit the sweet aroma of Jesus

Christ or a rotten stench. Your response to light, physical or spiritual, is either that of growth or ultimate death.

You choose to believe the One who is Truth, or you can believe in any of many false prophets. Einstein once remarked, "God doesn't play dice." In the final analysis it is your choice.

The final result is also binary: hell or heaven, a child of darkness or a child of light, in the book of death or in the book of life, eternal regret and punishment or everlasting wonder and joy beyond anything that we can imagine.

Sunlight / Sonlight

In many ways our physical world of sunlight is a binary world.

The Word of God makes it clear the world of Sonlight is a binary choice.

THINK AND GROW

1. It is a binary choice. In which condition are you?

2. Are you attracted or repelled by Sonlight?

15

Result:

Partakers of Light

We had completed the first part of our vacation. I shall never forget the look on the old gentleman's face.

My wife and I had spent several lovely days in Honolulu. This was the first vacation we had taken without our children. It seemed as if we had hiked or driven over every part of the Island of Oahu. Everything was going even better than we had planned. Just to think, the other islands were still to come.

Arriving at the Honolulu Airport, a major surprise greeted us. All inter-island flights for the rest of our trip had somehow been inadvertently canceled. After an hour or so of scurrying between the two major inter-island airlines and much discussion with the ticket agents and other personnel, we managed to have everything once again put in order. The only inconvenience was an additional hour's wait before we could leave Oahu bound for the Island of Kauai.

At last we were on board and the plane was just pulling away from the terminal when the flight attendant's voice sounded from the loudspeakers. "Good afternoon, ladies and gentlemen. We want to welcome you aboard Aloha Airlines, flight number 411 bound for the Island of Maui ..." Panic!

We were scheduled for Maui later in our trip, but our hotel and auto reservations for the next few days were on the Island of Kauai. After ever so much effort and double-checking, we must be on the wrong flight. I hadn't heard another word the flight attendant had said—all that routine safety information. Looking around I noticed mostly senior citizens wearing tour badges, and no one seemed disturbed. My wife leaned over into the aisle and asked a vibrant, grandfatherly-type gentleman across the aisle, "Sir, are you headed for Kauai or Maui?" He grinned from ear to ear; he was radiant. He motioned with both palms up and a shrug of his shoulders, then tilting his head toward the people in the row behind him, said, "I don't know, I'm with them!" This vibrant, content old gentleman may not have even known that he was in Hawaii. He had company, and he was happy.

The eventual outcome of the situation was that the flight attendant had been in error, so there was a happy ending.

Response to Light Summary

Some of the light that falls on an object is absorbed, some is refracted, and the remainder is reflected. Materials may be classified by how they react to light—as opaque, translucent, or transparent. Any one of these basic types of materials can produce an accurate image.

We have seen that artificial or substitute light distorts the true colors of an image. Mirages appear very real but produce a distorted image, and shadows reduce or distort the brightness of light.

Luminescent materials are found in animal, vegetable, and mineral classifications. We also saw that there are various possible binary reactions to light. All these concepts are interconnected in a variety of complex ways.

Different objects react differently to physical light. So too, different individuals react differently to spiritual light. The same sun that causes the desolation of the deserts provides life through germination in heavily vegetated areas. Just as surely, some men's hearts dry up and become as concrete-like dried mud when exposed to spiritual light, while others burst forth in newness of life through spiritual birth. Jesus

Christ said, "Do not marvel that I said to you, 'You must be born again'" (John 3:7).

The most basic, important, and unique property of light is that it allows us to see. Light manifests or makes visible. Paul wrote: "But everything exposed by the light becomes visible" (Ephesians 5:13 niv). Light is required for physical sight. Spiritual light from God allows spiritual understanding so that we can see and understand spiritual things.

Our ability to see is as much dependent upon the brain as it is on our eyes. We know that a person can be blind even though his eyes are perfect. The brain and eyes must work in harmony and unison if we are to experience physical sight.

To sense physical light, you must be alive and you must not be blind. To sense spiritual light, you must be spiritually alive and you must not be blinded by the Evil One. "The god of this age has blinded the minds of unbelievers, so that they cannot see the light of the glory of Christ Who is the image of God" (2 Corinthians 4:4 niv).

The Way

Since light reveals, it guides and protects. In the simple case of primitive man's nighttime fires, light was at once a revealer and a protector. Flashlights, auto headlights, and streetlights are all examples of light both revealing and protecting. Many a ship has been able to navigate the correct channel because of buoys and lighthouses. *Light shows the way.*

The Truth

Not only does light reveal the way, but it also reveals the truth. Light is an impartial judge. It reveals the beautiful and the ugly. Light reveals the innocent and the guilty. That is why crime rates are higher in the darkness hours. Light reveals the way and exposes danger. *Light reveals the truth.*

The Life

The secrets of our universe all seem to be connected intimately with light. It is light's revealing power that has allowed mankind to make great scientific discoveries. Chemistry, electricity, and all things are intricately related in complex ways to light. Einstein's formula, $E = mc^2$, clearly shows that all matter and all energy are related to light. Light is the secret to all of nature and all of life. Light in a remarkable way unlocks the truth about all things. Light reveals the way and exposes the truth; *light also provides life.*

The Way, the Truth, and the Life

"Jesus said to him [Thomas], *'I am the way, the truth, and the life.* No one comes to the Father except through Me" (John 14:6).

Our Total Dependence

We have previously seen how every living thing is dependent upon the light from our sun for its very existence. Light brings warmth and gives life. Without the sun this world as we know it would not exist. With light the grandeur of our environment is beyond human appreciation. David said, "The heavens declare the glory of God; and the firmament shows His handiwork. Day unto day utters speech, and night unto night reveals knowledge. There is no speech nor language where their voice is not heard. Their line has gone out through all the earth, and their words to the end of the world. In them He has set a tabernacle for the sun, which is like a bridegroom coming out of his chamber, and rejoices like a strong man to run its race. Its rising is from one end of heaven, and its circuit to the other end; and there is nothing hidden from its heat" (Psalm 19:1-6).

Not only is the sun the source of all life on earth but also the source of all the energy we use on earth. Light provides life and provides for the continuation of life. Jesus Christ said, "I am the light of the world. He who follows Me shall not walk in darkness, but have *the light of life*" (John 8:12).

Light reveals the way and guides in the correct way. Light exposes the truth, whether it is lovely or repulsive. Light is absolutely essential to our life on earth. Physical light shows the *way,* reveals the *truth,* and provides *life.* Speaking of the spiritual, Jesus Christ said, *"I am the way and the truth and the life.* No one comes to the Father except through Me" (John 14:6).

Application

Many parallels exist between the nature of physical light and the nature of spiritual light. As you have observed how objects react to physical light, you have seen analogies to the way humans respond to spiritual light.

One of the marvels of mankind is that we pass by the extraordinary without giving it a thought. At other times our existence is characterized by hours of pure trivia. It is as if modern man is deliberately willing to sacrifice the important on the altar of the inconsequential. Our priorities are often confused.

I once heard about a man who was wildly enthusiastic about his driving ability. He was taking a road trip with his wife. After traveling for many hours, his wife consulted a map and informed him that they were lost! The man replied cheerfully, "What's the difference? We're making good time!" This man and the elderly gentleman on the plane in Hawaii characterize much of mankind today—busy having a good time but with no concern regarding their destination.

Our final destination should be our most important priority. When "Doubting Thomas" approached our Lord following the Resurrection, he said, "Unless I see in His hands the print of the nails, and put my finger into the print of the nails, and put my hand into His side, I will not believe" (John 20:25). In God's economy faith is the first step; with God, believing provides seeing. Thomas was speaking for many when he said, "seeing is believing."

Do you understand all there is to know about physical light? (If you do, please let some of our scientists in on your knowledge.) Do you believe in physical light? What logic is it that refuses to believe the insurmountable evidence of spiritual light just because it is not fully understood?

Jesus Christ is the reality in this troubled world. We read regarding Paul's mission for Christ: "To open their eyes, in order to turn them from darkness to light, and from the power of Satan to God, that they may receive forgiveness of sins and an inheritance among those who are sanctified by faith in Me" (Acts 26:18). What is this inheritance which we may receive? We read, "His divine power has given to us all things that pertain to life and godliness, through the knowledge of Him who called us by glory and virtue, by which have been given to us exceedingly great and precious promises, that through these you may be partakers of the divine nature, having escaped the corruption that is in the world through lust" (2 Peter 1:3-4). We can be "partakers of the divine nature."

For those who are children of light, the challenge is clear: "For those who sleep, sleep at night, and those who get drunk are drunk at night. But let us who are of the day be sober, putting on the breastplate of faith and love, and as a helmet the hope of salvation" (1 Thessalonians 5:7-8). "The day of the Lord so comes as a thief in the night" (1 Thessalonians 5:2). "And do this, understanding the present time. The hour has come for you to wake up from your slumber, because salvation is nearer now than when we first believed. The night is nearly over; the day is almost here. So let us *put aside the deeds of darkness and put on the armor of light*. Let us behave decently, as in the daytime" (Romans 13:11-13 niv).

~ *Quote* ~ "Don't shine so that others can see you. Shine, so that through you, others can see Him." —C.S. Lewis

Sunlight / Sonlight

There are many parallels between the way physical objects react to sunlight and the way in which humans respond to Sonlight.

Perhaps the most important parallel is that both are often taken for granted.

THINK AND GROW

1. Do you typically accept your daily sunlight and all its benefits without much thought?

2. Do you typically live without real thought about Sonlight and all that He offers?

3. Have you embraced Sonlight?

4. Are you walking honestly as a child of the day?

16

The Bottom Line:

Light Heals!

Our subject is light—both natural sunlight and spiritual Sonlight. Spiritual light is as real as physical light. It would be a rare individual who would claim to have a complete understanding about God. It would perhaps be equally as rare to find someone who believed he knew all there is to know about physical light. The Bible says the following about God: "The King of kings and Lord of lords, who alone has immortality, *dwelling in unapproachable light*" (1 Timothy 6:15-16).

Physical life comes to us from the sun. Spiritual life comes to us from the Son. "There is therefore now no condemnation to those who are in Christ Jesus, who do not walk according to the flesh, but according to the Spirit. For the law of the Spirit of life in Christ Jesus has made me free from the law of sin and death" (Romans 8:1-2). Spiritual life flows through the child of God from the Spirit of God as a result of the work of the Son of God.

In the Book of Genesis we read that on the first day of the creation week, God caused light to appear. We are told in the Genesis account that God separated light from darkness. The physical light of the world revealed the grandeur of earth. When a person is born anew, becomes a new creation, the first thing wrought in his soul is spiritual light. The truth of God is revealed with its grandeur and beauty.

The visible light of the world is the sun—sunlight. Christ is the "Sun of righteousness"—Sonlight. One sun illuminates the entire world, and the Son of God illuminates all who are willing to have the blinders removed from their eyes. What the sun is in nature, the Son is in grace and glory to the believer. "Contact with God establishes within us a flow of the same type of energy that re-creates the world and renews springtime every year."[11]

Centuries ago the apostle John declared, "God is light and in Him is no darkness at all" (1 John 1:5). Only in recent times has man begun to learn about natural light and how to predict its behavior. We make use of this knowledge in the design of cameras, television, fiber optics, and lasers.

The Healing Power of Light

From earliest times man discovered that light is useful. For centuries the disinfectant properties have been known. Even today, many people prefer the freshness of clothes which have been dried in the sunlight over drying with mechanical means.

Light provides safety. Falls account for many injuries to humans, especially among the older segment of our population. Lighting reduces the numbers of falls. Today, scientists are studying how to make artificial lighting more healthful.

As we drive our vehicles brake lights and turn signals provide information for our safety. Traffic lights tell us to go, slow, or stop. Road signs communicate warnings.

Startling advances are being made in medicine in the use of light. Light can be used to improve our appearance. A variety of light therapies are used to remove hair, to regenerate dead follicles allowing increased hair growth, and to improve skin tone and texture. For example, Intense Pulsed Light (IPL) technology is used to rejuvenate skin as its light penetrates the skin. This technique can reduce redness, sun damage, pigmentation, scars, and stretch marks. Dermal Optical Thermolysis (DOT) is used to improve similar skin problems.

Today the technologies of fiber optics and lasers are involved in many branches of medicine. Light traveling through fiber optics provides vision inside the human body greatly improving diagnosis. Laser surgery has revolutionized medicine. Many kinds of surgery are now routinely done with lasers. One of the huge benefits to man has been a significant reduction in surgical incision size and the related correspondingly remarkable improvement in recovery time. It is clear that *light can also heal.*

Some researchers believe lighting in our homes, offices, and schools could be improved to help people stay healthy and productive by acting on their internal body clocks. The 24-hour internal body clock is best known for governing cycles of alertness and sleep, and for producing jet lag when people travel across time zones. Light cues, especially blue light, help keep the clock on its daily cycle.

One interesting medical advancement is the treatment of Seasonal Affective Disorder (SAD) patients. As far back as 400 B.C. the Greek physician Hippocrates observed that seasonal changes could cause physical and mental changes. In the early 1980s scientists at the National Institute of Mental Health recognized depression as a distinct, cyclical entity, and in 1987 the American Psychiatric Association deemed SAD a true affective (mood) disorder. This is a rare situation where recognition of an illness was nearly simultaneous with the discovery of a treatment: light therapy. SAD individuals do not regularly receive enough bright sunlight for their biological clocks to be triggered and reset. It is now known that most humans have a built-in clock that is not in synchronization with our 24-hour day but is closer to a 25-hour format. This is important because our internal clocks govern bodily rhythms including sleep. SAD patients can become starved for light, especially during winter months, and fall into depression. Most of us never see the effects because as we move about during daylight hours our internal clocks are reset. It is currently estimated that as many as five percent of North Americans suffer from SAD while an additional fifteen percent may have a mild form (the Winter Blues or Subsyndromal SAD). Today many SAD patients receive light therapy, often called *phototherapy,* in the form of bright light at spaced intervals to reset their biological clocks. Light therapy is a specialty—the color of light, the intensity, and even its aiming at the body are important. It is not an area for self-help without consulting a specialist. One specialist and professor of psychiatry has stated, "The benefit we're seeing is actually more than you would expect to see with antidepressant drugs in a comparable time period."[12]

Phototherapy is also currently being used as treatment in other situations such as jet lag, age related sleep disturbances, and for certain cancers (especially T-cell lymphoma), in a process called photopheresis. This process has also yielded some encouraging results in scleroderma (a disease in which the immune system attacks skin tissue), rheumatoid arthritis, and lupus. It is also being used experimentally in the treatment of juvenile diabetes and AIDS-related complex (ARC).

Our increasing knowledge of light affects not only medicine but also the consumer. In November of 1993 a South Korean electronics giant announced they had invented a "Bio Television" that converts television's electromagnetic beams into waves that produce a similar effect as sunlight on humans, animals, and plants. In their tests the longevity of fish and the freshness of flowers increased from 50 to 100 percent while kept near the Bio TV.

Physical light has great power to heal physically. Spiritual light has great power to heal spiritually. The Bible provides the answers which men seek regarding the knowledge of God. While it is true that no one fully understands God, we know that God exists and operates according to various principles. By studying God's written Word to man and by making use of what we learn, we can live more healthful, productive, and enjoyable lives.

Light is a form of energy and is the basis of all physical life on this planet we call earth. God is eternal and is the basis for all true spiritual life. "In Him was life, and the life was the light of men" (John 1:4).

Sunlight / Sonlight

Sunlight heals physically.

Sonlight heals spiritually.

THINK AND GROW

1. Have you ever realized benefits to your feelings of well-being (or perhaps even physical healing) from physical light?

2. Have you accessed the spiritual healing which is only found in Sonlight?

Epilog
The Majesty of Light:
Upward in a Flash

Einstein said, "The most beautiful thing we can experience is the mysterious. It is the source of all true art and all science." Sunlight is still not fully understood. Sonlight is not fully comprehended by even the children of light.

There are two stories about sunlight that have amused many. The first is about a class that had been taught about the tremendous speed of light that comes to us from the sun. The instructor was exclaiming the marvels of it all and then exclaimed, "Isn't it wonderful?" A voice from the back of the room replied, "It's not so great. After all, it's downhill all the way!"

The second is a comment that somebody once made. The substance of the comment was that the only thing that person knew about the speed of light was that he was glad it was becoming the time of year when light doesn't arrive so early in the morning!

These two anecdotes may make us smile, and we might be critical of anyone who seems so careless regarding understanding the reality of light. It is tragic that so many are equally careless when it comes to understanding or investigating the reality of spiritual light. Unfortunately, some of us have not applied what understanding we do have of God in the same meticulous way that we have applied our understanding of physical light.

Part of the reason is that just as the physically dead person cannot perceive light, the spiritually dead person cannot perceive God. It requires physical birth to be sensitive to physical light, and it requires spiritual birth to be sensitive to spiritual light.

Those who perceive both physical and spiritual light realize that the two are intricately interwoven. For example, physical light, as we have seen, is related in a very basic way to all matter and energy. Concerning Jesus Christ, we read, "in Him all things hold together" (Colossians 1:17 niv), and "in Him we live and move and have our being" (Acts 17:28).

Those who have had a spiritual birth are reminded, "now *you are* light in the Lord. Live as children of light" (Ephesians 5:8), "that you may proclaim the praises of Him who called you out of darkness into His marvelous light" (1 Peter 2:9).

There is coming a time when Jesus Christ will return to earth. Listen to how Matthew describes the second coming of Christ: "For as the lightning comes from the east and flashes to the west, so also will the coming of the Son of Man be" (Matthew 24:27).

Light travels at a speed that would enable seven trips around the earth in one second. Light can circle this planet faster than you or I can wink. Jesus Christ has promised to return to earth for His church "in a flash" (1 Corinthians 15:52 niv). And "we know that when He is revealed, we shall be like Him" (1 John 3:2). Jesus Christ will be the visible light in all His glory in the new creation.

While suggesting some of the ways that our understanding of physical light allows us to more fully understand God, we have tried to understand what John meant when he was inspired by the Holy Spirit of God to write "God is light." It is the author's sincere prayer that each reader is able to say with John, "We have seen His glory" (John 1:14 niv), but always remembering "now we see in a mirror, dimly, but then face to face. Now I know in part, but then I shall know just as I also am known" (1 Corinthians 13:12).

THINK AND GROW

Are you walking in the light or just living in the light?

Please Consider This

If you liked this book, please leave a review online. Reviews help the authors you appreciate get recognized and help other readers choose what to read.

About the Author

Robert Lloyd Russell

Biography

Robert Lloyd Russell's books have won national and international literary awards including a World Book Award (one of just three awards across all genres). He is the editor of a book containing transcribed spoken messages of martyred missionary Jim Elliot. As a small boy Robert lived in the Elliot home at a time prior to Jim's departure for the mission field. The transcriptions were carefully made from old wire recordings, the forerunner of magnetic tape recordings. Jim was one of Robert's Sunday School teachers and Jim's father was one of his spiritual mentors.

Russell has a diverse secular background which spans many functions including engineering, manufacturing, sales, marketing, and staff positions. His technical career included the management of a wide variety of engineers, physicists, and scientists in the high-technology industry.

During the 1970s while he was Camera Engineering Manager for a Fortune 500 corporation, he became fascinated with the attributes of light and the parallels to the attributes of God. He would later write about these parallels in some of his books.

In the early 1970s a senior executive of a major corporation began seeking Robert's opinions and advice. This was the start of a part-time consulting business. Then, from 1990 until his retirement in 2005, Robert devoted his entire career to advising and coaching many executives in a variety of organizations. Based in Portland, Oregon, his consulting practice routinely provided coaching and counseling on a wide range of business issues including ethics, overall effectiveness and profitability, organizational cultural issues, and Total Quality concepts.

During the 1980s as an active Christian businessman concerned about ethics, Robert enrolled in seminary and earned a Master of Christian Leadership degree from Western Seminary. For many years he was a popular adult Sunday School and Bible Study teacher.

Robert refers to himself as a simple **A-B-C** kind of guy: Christian **A**uthor, Christian **B**logger, and Christian **C**onsultant and **C**oach. His blog entitled "Abundant Life Now[1]" has been read in nearly 200 countries and translated into more than 100 languages.

---

1. http://robertlloydrussell.blogspot.com/

Want Free Books?

As an author, I want to thank you for reading *SAMSON: Spirit-Filled to Self-Centered"* and I

regard the feedback of my readers very highly.

When considering buying a book many people weigh reviews carefully before deciding to purchase. If you enjoyed this book, would you consider assisting me by helping others make an informed decision? Leaving a review (even just a star rating without commentary) can help spread the message of the Gospel and increase others' faith through these books. It is also a great way to support this international ministry.

||||| |||||

Robert Lloyd Russell's Newsletter[1]

Sign up for occasional updates from author Robert Lloyd Russell: https://www.subscribepage.com/rlr

He is committed to not bothering you with frequent newsletters. When he does send out occasional communications, it will contain one or more of the following:

- Advance information about current projects
- Related news
- Prayer requests
- Notification of **FREE eBooks** for a limited time
- Other items which may be of interest

---

1. https://www.subscribepage.com/rlr

(If you decide you no longer want to receive the newsletter, you may take advantage of the "unsubscribe" option at the bottom of each email.)

|||||

Robert Lloyd Russell's eBooks are available from your favorite online eBook retailer.

You may also want to visit the author's book website Books by Robert Lloyd Russell that lists his eBooks and printed books along with additional information, (booksrlr), or go to Books to Read[2] (https://books2read.com/ap/81Ym5B/Robert-Lloyd-Russell).

|||||

You are invited to connect with Robert Lloyd Russell through his daily internet blog *Abundant Life Now*[3] for inspiration and insight. (http://robertlloydrussell.blogspot.com/)

---

2. https://books2read.com/ap/81Ym5B/Robert-Lloyd-Russell

3. *http://RobertLloydRussell.blogspot.com/*

What To Read Next

"GOD'S NATURE: Sonlight—Sunlight" ISBN: 978-1393359371 ~ ASIN: B083L97PZV

An easy-to-read devotional style book which presents new and unforgettable insights. This landmark book identifies fascinating parallels between natural and spiritual light. Analogies teach profound truth in simple language.

"First there was Tozer with *The Knowledge of the Holy,* and then Packer gave us *Knowing God,* and now Russell has taken us further." —Dr. Earl D. Radmacher, General Editor, Nelson Study Bible/New King James Study Bible

Note: This eBook is an update of the first two sections of an earlier print book *GOD LIGHT: Sunlight Sonlight,* which **won six awards.**

Choose your favorite eBook retailer

https://books2read.com/GodsNature

"GOD'S CHILD: Like a Tree" ISBN: 978-1393518266 ~ ASIN: B0874CHLD7

Dr. Ronald B. Allen, a nationally recognized expert on the Psalms, described this book as "The definitive work on Psalm 1."

A timely book for those who long for faster, more consistent spiritual growth. In today's Christian communities many are complacent in their ultimate destination and they neglect the importance of the journey. In so doing, they miss out on many of the here and now benefits of their adoption into the family of God. The normal (not average) Christian is growing more like Jesus Christ as they continue their life on earth. If you long to be a disciple who pleases God, this book is for you. This book is extremely relevant to today's culture.

Choose your favorite eBook retailer

https://books2read.com/GodsChild

"GOD'S CHURCH: Christ's Pearl" ISBN: 978-1393268093 ~ ASIN: B07XFPMVQT

Early in the book the author provides a straightforward look at the three most popular interpretations of the parable of the pearl of great price. Included is a clear Bible-based rejection of the common notion that the pearl represents salvation.

The major portion of the work provides parallels between the "one pearl of great price" and the Christian Church. Presented are seven unique aspects of a pearl which parallel the uniqueness of the Church. Finally, eight additional characteristics of a pearl and their parallels are presented.

Note: This eBook is an update of an earlier print book *ONE PRECIOUS PEARL: God's Design for His Church,* which **won five awards**.

Choose your favorite eBook retailer

https://books2read.com/GodsChurch

"CHRIST'S DISCIPLE: How To Finish Strong" ISBN: 978-1393844402 ~ ASIN: B091XZF79B

Written for those who long for faster, more consistent spiritual growth. Many in today's Christian communities are complacent about their ultimate destination and they neglect the importance of the journey. In so doing, they miss out on many of the here and now benefits of their adoption into the family of God. The normal (not average) Christian is growing more like Jesus Christ as they continue their life on earth. If you long to be a disciple who pleases God, this book is for you.

Choose your favorite eBook retailer

https://books2read.com/ChristsDisciple

"GOD'S DESIRE: How To Please God" ISBN: 978-1393211785 ~ ASIN: B08H4F619W

This book develops two graphic models. The "Christian Life Model" is about victorious Christian living. Included in this section are the author's detailed acrostics for fellowship, obedience, power, prayer, witness, and the Word.

The "Christian Guidance Model" shows the interrelationship of the "Christian Life Model" and one's inner convictions, Godly counsel, and the Lordship of Jesus Christ.

Note: This eBook is an update of an earlier print book "*THY WILL BE DONE ON EARTH: Understanding God's Will for You.*"

Choose your favorite eBook retailer

https://books2read.com/GodsDesire

"GOD'S LIGHT: How To Respond" ISBN: 978-1393424994

An easy-to-read devotional style book which identifies parallels between the reactions of physical objects to natural light and the reactions of humans to spiritual light. These analogies teach profound truth in simple language.

Written in short easily digestible segments, it is ideal reading for the person on the go. Readers gain a greater appreciation regarding Christians shining like lights.

Note: This eBook is an update of the third section of an earlier print book *GOD LIGHT: Sonlight Sunlight,* which won **six awards**.

Choose your favorite eBook retailer

https://books2read.com/GodsLight

"CHRIST'S BLOOD: 7+ Amazing Benefits" ISBN: 979-8201460877 ~ ASIN: B098W6LHVM

Understand the direct benefits to *you* from Christ's death and resurrection.

There are seven (plus one) directly stated benefits in Scripture.

Ponder ten additional benefits resulting from the Cross.

Choose your favorite eBook retailer

https://books2read.com/ChristsBlood

"TEMPTATION" 50+ Tips" ISBN: 979-8201564209 ~ ASIN: B0BCPN5YGW

Everyone is tempted (even Christ was)

50+ practical tips for personal victory over temptation!

Understand the battle and your spiritual weapons

Overcome the types of temptations you will face

Be confident and victorious in your Christian life

Choose your favorite eBook retailer

https://books2read.com/temptation-50tips

"PRIDE: Good and Bad" ISBN: 979-8201002053 ~ ASIN: B09SGSQLH9

Achieve a more consistent Christian life

As humans, we all have a common problem. Like rust to steel, pride is to our lives. Although there are examples of good pride in the Bible, most of the time pride is a negative part of our being.

Understanding the problem of pride is a vital part of gaining consistent spiritual victory as we live our daily lives.

Choose your favorite eBook retailer

https://books2read.com/Pride-Good-and-Bad

"SAMSON: Spirit-Controlled to Self-Centered" ISBN: 979-8215866122 ~ ASIN: B0BSZZSY8J

The Biblical account of Samson's life includes ten significant victories interspersed among fifteen problematic events. How can we avoid a spiritually fickle life?

What are the commonalities and contrasts between the lives of Samson and Christ? How did God evaluate Samson's life?

What practical lessons can we apply to our daily activities by looking at his life?

Choose your favorite eBook retailer

https://books2read.com/samson-robert-lloyd-russell

"*PETER: Failure to Faith*" ISBN: 979-8223422327 ~ ASIN: B0CBBC7DZC

Follow Peter's life in chronological order as he progresses from a fickle follower to a dynamic disciple.

This book can easily be a *fast read*. Due to small segments, it can also be used for *daily devotions* or in *short segments* by busy individuals. For scholars it can be the basis for a *lengthy personal study*. Small groups use it as a *spur to discussions*. Whatever your choice, enjoy as you read and reflect!

Choose your favorite eBook retailer

https://books2read.com/Peter-Failure-to-Faith

"JIM ELLIOT: Recorded Messages" ISBN: 978-1393887959 ~ ASIN: B088FZ3XSC

Note: This eBook is an updated and significantly expanded version of an earlier print book *"JIM ELLIOT: A Christian Martyr Speaks to You."*

Jim Elliot's spoken words transcribed for you – six practical messages with amazing depth and insight. These messages were given by this martyred Christian missionary before he left for the mission field in Ecuador. They were transcribed from a wire recorder, a forerunner of the magnetic tape recorder.

Christians of all maturity levels benefit from the understanding gained from Jim's discussions.

Choose your favorite eBook retailer

https://books2read.com/JimElliot

Print Book: ISBN: 978-0741475534 ~ *"GOD LIGHT: Sunlight Sonlight"* <u>won six awards</u> and is an easy-to-read devotional style book which presents new and unforgettable insights. This book identifies fascinating parallels between natural and spiritual light, and provides applications of natural and spiritual light. Analogies teach profound truth in simple language.

Available wherever quality print books are sold.

Note: There is an eBook update of the first two sections of this book entitled: *"GOD'S NATURE: Sonlight Sunlight."* The third section of this book is updated in the eBook entitled: *"GOD'S LIGHT: How To Respond."* Both are listed previously.

Print Book: ISBN: 978-0741462329 ~ ***ONE PRECIOUS PEARL: God's Design for His Church*** <u>won five awards.</u>

A straightforward look at the three most common interpretations of this parable.

The major portion of the book provides parallels between the "one pearl of great price" and the Christian Church.

Available wherever quality print books are sold.

Note: There is an eBook update of this book is entitled "*GOD'S CHURCH: Christ's Pearl.*" It is listed previously.

Print Book: ISBN: 978-1606474310 ~ *"THY WILL BE DONE ON EARTH: Understanding God's Will for You"* is for those who are serious about living life in a way that pleases God.

Through the development of two graphic models the author provides insights regarding the interrelationship of fundamentals of the Christian faith.

Available wherever quality print books are sold.

Note: There is an eBook update of this book entitled *"GOD'S DESIRE: How To Please God."* It is listed previously.

Print Book: ISBN: 978-1615797646 ~ *"JIM ELLIOT: A Christian Martyr Speaks To You"* is directly relevant to all Christians.

Those with an interest in the history of missions or current missions will find the book riveting.

All Christians will appreciate Jim's straightforward, hard-hitting style of speaking.

Available wherever quality print books are sold.

Note: There is an eBook update of this book entitled *"JIM ELLIOT: Recorded Messages."* It has been enhanced and expanded with two additional messages and is listed previously.

Bibliography

Bragg, Sir William, O.M., K.B.E., D.SC., F.R.S.; *The Universe of Light*; New York, The Macmillan Company; 1933.

Calder, Nigel; *Einstein's Universe*; New York: The Viking Press; 1979.

Collis, John Stewart; *The World of Light*: New York: Horizon Press: 1960.

Cook, J. Gordan; *We Live By the Sun*; New York: The Dial Press; 1957.

Hurvich, Leo N.; *Color Vision*; Sunderland, MA: Sinauer Associates Inc.; 1981.

Jenkins, Francis A. & White, Harvey E.; *Fundamentals of Optics*; 4th Edition; McGraw-Hill; 1976.

Klein, H. Arthur; *Bioluminescence*; Philadelphia/New York: J. B. Lippincott Co.; 1965.

Minnaert, M.; *The Nature of Light and Color in the Open Air*; New York: Dover Publications, Inc.; 1954.

Morris, Richard; *Light*; Indianapolis/New York: The Bobbs-Merrill Co., Inc.; 1979.

Ruchlis, Hy.; *The Wonder of Light: A Picture Story of How and Why We See*; New York: Harper & Brothers; 1960.

Sagan, Carl; *Cosmos*; New York: Random House; 1980.

Sanders, J. H.; *Velocity of Light*; New York: Pergamon Press; 1965.

Sheard, Charles, Ph.D., Sc.D.; *Life-Giving Light*; New York: The Century Co.; 1933.

Smith, Warren J.; *Modern Optical Engineering: The Design of Optical Systems*; McGraw-Hill; 1966.

Smithsonian Exposition Books; *Fire of Life*; New York: W. W. Norton & Co.; 1981.

[1] Sheard, Charles, Ph.D., Sc.D., *Life-Giving Light* (New York The Century Co., 1933), page 112.

[2] Needham, David C., *Birthright: Christian, Do You Know Who You Are?* (Portland, Oregon: Multnomah Press, 1979), pages 74-75.

[3] Ibid, page 93.

[4] Ibid, pages 94-95.

[5] Collis, John Stewart, *The World of Light* (New York: Horizon Press, 1960), page 105.

[6] Bounds, E. M., *Purpose in Prayer* (Grand Rapids, Michigan: Book House, 1920), page 142.

[7] Klein, H. Arthur, *Bioluminescence* (Philadelphia/New York: J. B. Lippincott Co., 1965), page 171.

[8] Sagan, Carl, *Cosmos* (New York: Random House, 1980), page 278.

[9] Cook, J. Gordan, *We Live By the Sun* (New York: The Dial Press, 1957), page 189.

[10] Taylor, Ron and Valerie, *Paradise Beneath the Sea*, National Geographic, Vol. 159, No. 5, May 1981, pages 653 and 658.

[11] Peale, Norman Vincent, *The Power of Positive Thinking* (Greenwich, Conn.: Fawcett Publications, Inc., 1952).

[12] Daniel Kripke, M.D., Professor of Psychiatry, University of California at San Diego. He has been using light therapy at the Veterans Affairs Medical Center in San Diego since 1981.

Don't miss out!

Visit the website below and you can sign up to receive emails whenever Robert Lloyd Russell publishes a new book. There's no charge and no obligation.

https://books2read.com/r/B-A-QQUI-MVBKB

Also by Robert Lloyd Russell

Bible Character Series
Samson: Spirit-Controlled to Self-Centered
Peter: Failure to Faith

Christian Concepts Series
God's Church: Christ's Pearl
God's Nature: Sonlight Sunlight
God's Child: Like a Tree

Christian Growth Series
God's Desire: How To Please God
God's Light: How To Respond
Christ's Disciple: How To Finish Strong

Christian Theology Series
Christ's Blood: 7+ Amazing Benefits
Pride: Good and Bad
Temptation: 50+ Tips